COWGIRL POWER

COWGIRL POWER

How to Kick Ass in Business and Life

GAY GADDIS

CENTER STREET

New York Nashville

CONTENTS

PREFACE

You may not know it, but there is a cowgirl within you. I wrote this book because of the strength, courage, and life lessons I have learned from historic cowgirls and modern day cowgirls, and I couldn't wait to share these inspirational stories with you to help you find your own unique, personal power.

By finding and understanding your personal power, you can achieve more than you have ever imagined. As you read this book, put all of the negativity about women's success, or lack of, behind you, and look to a bold future.

My goal for each reader is to help you understand and gain your unique personal power. Why? Because it will give you more choices and opportunities throughout your life. It will minimize your fears and give you the strength and courage to grab the brass ring when it comes around.

You may ask, what do historic cowgirls have to teach us in this day and age? I hope you will come to admire these cowgirls and the women who have blazed a trail for you.

Cowgirls have a braveness, authenticity, and grit that I see reflected in powerful women today. I come from a long line of cowgirls. My mother was a cowgirl. My mother-in-law was a cowgirl. They were tough, strong people who grew up during the heyday of America's cowgirl superstars in the 1920s and 1930s. These cowgirls, and their inner strength, are symbols and guides for the challenges we face today.

As I look back at how I built my advertising agency, T3, from the ground up I think we intuitively understood this. I can see it now and want to help others understand how we created a unique culture that empowers people—men and women as equal partners in navigating this thing called life with grace and love.

Thanks to our three children, Ben, Rebecca, Sam, and my husband, Lee Gaddis, for putting up with a hard-charging Texas woman and being inspirational leaders in their own right. Thanks to my friends and extended family for their un-wavering support.

My heartfelt thanks to the wonderful people I have had the privilege to work with at T3 through the years. We have learned so much together. You have all taught me the power of talented, creative, strong people who genuinely care about each other. And to the many clients who put their careers and companies in our hands, and for the mutual trust and respect we have shared.

I made the decision not to name T3 employees in this book, simply because there are too many. So I honor you all instead.

This book is dedicated to Lee. He is my true partner in all aspects of business and life. A mentor, champion, humorist, Texas cowboy rancher, and a big character! We make things happen in miraculous ways.

COWGIRL POWER

Bonnie McCarroll thrown from Silver
(Historic Photo Archive/Getty Images)

INTRODUCTION

This is one of the most famous images in cowgirl history. It was taken during the 1915 Pendleton Round-Up in Oregon and shows Bonnie McCarroll being thrown in the heat of competition by a horse named Silver. She just sums up the determination, grit, and competitive nature of cowgirls, and that is what this book is all about. How can we all draw upon their courage and find our own personal power to be able to kick ass in our careers and lives?

Bonnie embodies all of this and more. In 1922, she went on to win the cowgirl bronc riding championship at Cheyenne Frontier Days and at the first Madison Square Garden Rodeo. She grew up on a small stage and wasn't afraid to scale up to the big stage. She fearlessly and boldly performed before kings, queens, and presidents. After being thrown, she climbed back on and continued to perform. She never, never gave up, and even died trying to compete on a wild bronc in 1929.

If you walk into the rotunda at the National Cowgirl Museum and Hall of Fame in Fort Worth, Texas, you see amazing images and exhibits about historic cowgirls like Bonnie

McCarroll. If you look closely throughout the rotunda, you will see words that define who these women were.

Admired. Fearless. Visionary. Steadfast. Dependable. Original. Resourceful. Bold. Clever. Genuine. Skillful. True. Dauntless. Adventurous. Focused. Independent. Confident. Creative. Dedicated. Hardworking. Spirited. Trustworthy. Determined. Honored. Earnest. Passionate. Natural. Celebrated. Authentic.

I have read those words over and over again. They are the perfect definition of cowgirl power. It was true for our historic cowgirls. It is true today. You just need to reach down into your gut and pull it out. Cowgirl power is about taking responsibility for yourself and finding the personal power that is within you. It slaps down the traditional, sometimes negative, definitions of power and says by finding your inner personal power you open up a world of possibilities.

Cowgirls, my true heroines, are our trail guides through this book. Each chapter begins with a profile of a cowgirl, teaching us by her example about her own wonderful strengths and power. I also share my own stories to show you how I found my personal power. And, each step of the way, from my childhood through my early career, and later as an experienced CEO and leader, I give you guidance on how to do it in your own unique way.

All of this unfolds as I tell my stories. It is real-life success and failure told with a lot of candor, heart, and good old Texas humor. I encourage you to read the book with sticky notes or a big highlighter. Nothing would make me happier than to see your book with lots of flags and notes written in the margins. I encourage you to flag things that resonate with you. All of these ideas are where I gained my personal power. Not all of them will be right for you. But I guarantee some will touch you deeply.

The last section of the book is the Cowgirl Toolkit, and it

condenses most of the big ideas in the book into brief summaries. Compare the notes you took while reading the book and see which ideas apply to you now, or maybe a few months or years from now.

This book is not about changing you. You are just fine. It is about understanding your strengths, building on them, valuing them, and giving yourself credit for what you have achieved and what you will achieve. I do not tell you what you should do. If you want to stay home and raise your children, that's great. If you want to build a distinguished career, that's great. If you want to do both, I'm all for it. What I can give you is the ability to see yourself and build your personal power, which will result in you filling buckets and buckets full of goodwill. That goodwill will create so many opportunities for you so, no matter what you do, you will have lots and lots of amazing options.

Bessie Herberg portrait
(Buffalo Bill Center of the West, Cody, Wyoming, USA; P.6.0611)

Chapter 1

PERSONAL POWER IS THE ANSWER

Bessie Herberg's portrait embodies the essence of cowgirl power. She looks you straight in the eye, walks in with her hat firmly planted on her head, and exudes a sense of personal style and fashion. While many of the cowgirls in this book are pretty rough-and-tumble types, Bessie tells us that it is OK to be a bit of a fashionista if it helps your career and, of course, if it is authentically you. I can tell you, Bessie was authentic! Her character, appearance, and talents gave her personal power.

She is also one of the more than 450 women who worked for Wild West shows and rodeos between the 1890s and the1930s. These cowgirls were among the first professional athletes in the United States. They learned their horseback riding and roping skills while growing up on farms and ranches, doing the same work as their fathers and brothers.

When the opportunity came to travel, and make the big time, in many cases on an international stage, they didn't blink an eye. They were decisive and said, "Let 'er rip!" They rode in the arena and competed with anyone on the rodeo circuit. When recognizing the best of the best, these gals didn't let gender get in the way of a win. They drew on their own personal power and led the way for us all.

As I studied the powerful cowgirls of our past, I was energized and emboldened, yet humbled. They provide just the kind of role models I believe we can all learn from. The cowgirls will inspire you and help you see a path that perhaps you hadn't seen before. Let them be your guides. Let them speak to you like no one else can, through their courage, kindness and deeds, competitiveness and authenticity.

CHALLENGES WOMEN FACE IN THE WORKPLACE TODAY

I wrote this book because I wanted to help today's women, especially young women, find more of my cowgirls' strength and personal power in their work and family life. I have watched young mothers go through their pregnancies and then face the realities of having a job and a new baby. I have seen very capable women not be as forceful about managing their careers as their male counterparts. I have seen women lose their ambition to take C-suite leadership roles. But I have also seen women who somehow managed it all and succeeded beyond all measure. Why does it work well for some and not so well for others?

I have spent a lot of my time over the past ten years encouraging women to pursue careers in business. I am a member of Paradigm for Parity (P4P)—a coalition of women who want to speed up the pace of gender parity in C-suites and on boards. In 2016, P4P published a white paper, which is a thoughtful list of recommendations of changes that business leaders should make to help the cause. I have attended countless seminars on women's issues, discussing changes that need to be made. I wholeheartedly support all of these initiatives.

But I am struck by one thing; none of these initiatives say anything about what women need to do to help themselves. All of the recommendations in the Paradigm for Parity white paper[1] are things that others should do. There are no recommendations for individual women. The research studies and magazine articles about women's pay, admission to the C-suites, and being passive and not assertive are endless. They are the most powerful indicator of what is wrong. They do not ask women to buck up. That creates a huge gaping hole in the dialogue. For women to excel in their careers, they need to take on most of the responsibility themselves. By only focusing on what other people should do, they weaken their credibility.

That is not the cowgirl way.

As I researched the issues, I found other challenges women face. Women say they have a hard time seeing themselves as leaders. They struggle with their self-confidence. *Fortune*, the *New York Times*, *Forbes*, and *Inc.* all have countless stories about women's lack of confidence. Women's issues with hesitating to ask for deserved promotions and equitable pay are well known.

Here are these smart, capable women who are struggling with work–life balance issues, issues about their inner strength. They have trouble seeing themselves as leaders. Many are dissatisfied with their senior leadership at work. Many are dissatisfied with the work environment and culture.

My problem with all of this is that no personal solutions are ever offered. The most frequent recommendations are that management needs to try harder, recruit more, and do better training. That companies should put more value on diversity. People have been advocating all of that for twenty years with little, if any, impact. I even read one article entitled "7 Ways to Build Your Confidence" that suggested women eat better and exercise more. Give me a break!

The more I thought about it, the more perplexed I got. Why have women not excelled as well as men in the work environment? Why are there so few senior women executives and so few women board members of major corporations when women outnumber men today in college educations and perform well academically?

At first, I thought, it has to be the baby thing. Women have babies as their careers start to develop, and babies come along and derail the career. However, I realize that there are many successful working mothers, so we cannot put all of the emphasis on children being the root cause of women's apparent lack of success.

I have been a can-do, confident, and a little outrageous person my whole life. So why did I not experience this lack of self-confidence, when so many other women do? Where did my moxie come from? I just powered through the baby issues. Sure, it was tough and challenging, but I never considered leaving the business world. Not once.

As I worked through these questions, I began to see all of these issues as symptoms of a larger issue. I came to one simple revelation—that we all have been talking about the wrong issue. All of these challenges are symptoms, not the real problem. The real problem is that many women do not understand how to build and use personal power as instinctively as men do.

WHAT IS PERSONAL POWER?

Max Weber defined power as "the ability to control others, events, or resources; to make happen what one wants to happen in spite of obstacles, resistance, or opposition."[2]

Our traditional perception about power in business comes

from authority, hierarchy, almost a military-like top-down approach to business. For some situations, like the military, that works great. But for today's collaborative, creative economy, it can be counterproductive at best.

The power I am describing is not bestowed on you by someone else, it comes from within yourself. It comes from inspiration, charisma, and leadership. It comes from friendship, teamwork, an open heart, and an abundance of goodwill. It comes from humor and character and grit.

We will not find our power reciting statistics about how little progress we have made. Or harping on lack of direction or mentorship. Or lecturing on what someone else should do. We will find our power with our skills that are perfectly aligned with the drivers of today's economy—collaboration, innovation, and emotional intelligence.

We will find our power in financial success, profits. Power in imagination, creativity. In empathy, mentoring, leading. Power is there for the taking, and more often than not it comes from connecting with people and offering a hand up. This is a vast, largely untapped source of power for women to draw on that is completely natural, authentic, abundant, and accessible to all, regardless of their position in life.

I am advocating a more thoughtful, strategic approach to building personal power and believe it is the single most important issue facing women and their careers today. This is a new perspective to see our skills, emotions, and intellect in ways that help women appreciate their innate strengths and build upon them. This new perspective about what personal power is will enable women to take on the business world with confidence, self-assurance, and moxie by being who they really are.

When women learn to see these strengths in themselves,

they will quickly see that they are just as capable as the men in their organizations, perhaps more so.

WHY IS POWER IMPORTANT?

If you understand business negotiations, you know the answer. Most of your interactions with people in your life are negotiations. Maybe not negotiations in the classic business sense, but negotiations nonetheless. Where are we going to lunch? Are we going to have children? Where are we going on vacation? I deserve a promotion and a raise; do you agree?

We all know it is best to negotiate from a position of strength. You can find strength if you change your perception about what personal power is.

Let me give you an example. There is a guy at my company who has invited every new employee to lunch during their first week on the job for over ten years. No one ever asked him to do it, he just did. He had no authority, no direct reports. But by his act of kindness and genuine interest in people, he became one of the most respected, powerful people in our company. He always knew more about what was going on than anyone else. There is an old saying in Texas, "If an owl tells you something, you can take it to the bank." He earned that same authority.

Someone told me recently that personal power is all the things you do at work that are not in your job description. That sums it up pretty well.

Cowgirl power is about developing what already exists in you. It is not a quick or easy answer. It does not get around hard work and dealing with tough issues. It is not a shortcut. But it is about taking personal responsibility for yourself and not being too reliant on others. It is about methodically building your skills and knowledge so that you get better and better. Growing your competencies is the only authentic way to become authentically assertive.

I am not advocating that all women should pursue challenging business careers. I admire moms who choose to stay at home and focus their energy on their kids. Some of those moms start their own small businesses that give them a lot of flexibility. Many are the backbone of our communities, serving as volunteers across so many worthy organizations that could not exist without them. Still other women enjoy their jobs without having aspirations of taking on executive leadership responsibilities. Many of them have different values that are not compatible with the C-suite. I get it.

Building your personal power increases your options. What you want to do with your life is your decision. I want you to have many wonderful choices at every stage of your life.

Three girls and Mandy, second from left, riding sidesaddle
(Gaddis Family Photo Collection)

Chapter 2

FINDING MY OWN POWER—THE EARLY DAYS

My husband's grandmother, Florence Chiles, was a cowgirl. This photograph is from about 1885. Florence is the little girl third from the left. The older woman next to her was a beloved ranch employee named Mandy. She was part African American and part Native American. Everyone in the photograph is riding sidesaddle, the proper thing to do, and they are all dressed in petticoats and bonnets to protect them from the harsh South Texas sun.

Mandy took care of the little girls and took them riding often. They would ride out of sight from the house, and Mandy would let them climb down, unsaddle their horses, take off their petticoats and bonnets, and ride the horses bareback like circus performers. They did tricks, raced each other, and developed into accomplished cowgirls. When they were done, they would put on their saddles and petticoats and ride demurely home. They never got caught.

Florence died at seventy-five years old, but all her life she told stories about Mandy and how much the girls loved her. Florence wrote down the many stories of her life growing up that have been passed down like fine heirlooms. We cherish and learn from them still today. Mandy helped those three little girls find their personal power.

This chapter is about my true stories of some of the high points and low points of my life. I take you through them because I want to show you how and where I began to develop my personal power. It is an important perspective because, as you will see, success is not a straight line. You will see how I formed the principles that have guided my life, step-by-step. I hope they help you realize when you reach a pivotal point in your life.

GROWING UP IN EAST TEXAS

I grew up in Liberty, a small town in East Texas, where I learned a very powerful value system of ethics, honesty, hard work, and a remarkable sense of community. I was a cowgirl as a little girl and have always loved cowgirls' power, strength, determination, and courage. Their values and spirit are my inspiration for this book.

My mother, Dottie Warren, was a cowgirl herself. But at twelve years old, she lost her right arm to cancer. She had always been right-handed. After the operation her parents babied her and everyone felt sorry for her. One day, after she recovered from the surgery, her high school typing teacher called her out into the hall and said, "Dorothy, it is your choice. You can be depressed and be a cripple all your life, or you can put yourself out there and be all you can be." That advice had a major effect on her, and probably even more on me.

Mother put herself out there and never looked back. Now as I look at her life, I only remember her being unable to do two things because of her arm: She could not cook large holiday meals and could not sew. But she found a solution for both.

She could do almost anything. (Her college roommates said she rolled her own hair and tied her shoes.) She typed, played the piano and tennis, and had a set of "one" golf club. She played cards, taught embroidery classes to little girls, and never, never complained. Most people didn't even notice her missing arm until perhaps weeks or years after they met her, because she would cleverly and casually throw a sweater or jacket around her shoulders. She was an incredibly strong and powerful person, and coming across as an invalid just wasn't who she was. Any power and strength I have today comes from my mother. *Dottie Warren was a cowgirl.*

My dad, Gene Warren, was in World War II and saw combat in the South Pacific. After the war he got a civil engineering degree and moved to Texas with my mom to find opportunity in the booming Texas oil fields. After a few years he opened his own land surveying business, Warren Engineering. He wore a Stetson hat, a pair of khaki pants, and cowboy boots to his office. When he was in the field doing survey work, the Stetson came off and cowboy boots were replaced by rubber boots. He would come home covered in mud and would undress outside and then head to the bathroom in his underwear. He would draw a hot bath and then pour in some Pine-Sol to kill the ticks and chiggers. He'd soak there with his cigarettes and beer and listen to St. Louis Cardinals baseball games on the radio.

My mom had her own kindergarten, Warren Kindergarten. She was a beloved teacher who taught thousands of kids how to read. She was everyone's favorite teacher and had a unique way of connecting with kids, regardless of their status in life.

THE COWGIRL WAY

Almost as soon as I could walk, my dad would dress me up in a cowgirl outfit with boots and a hat and a little leather coat trimmed with fringe. He would take me downtown and show off his little cowgirl at Layl's diner, where some of the biggest oil deals in Texas were made. I, of course, was the center of attention and took full advantage of it!

It was my godfather, Felton Dennison, who made me a real cowgirl. He put me on a horse, and by the time I was six I was riding with him working cattle. I called him Uncle Felton, and he and I would ride for hours through the rice fields checking on the livestock. He always treated me as a grown-up, never as a little girl. His respect toward me has stayed with me all my life and gave me much of my confidence. He taught me so much. In Texas, we call people like Felton Dennison "the salt of the earth."

My godmother and Felton's wife, Elouise, was a saint. She stepped in for Dottie when it came time to prepare the big holiday meals. (I still use her recipe for Thanksgiving dressing to this day.) And she could sew like nobody's business. One of her greatest acts of love for me was hand-sewing thousands of sequins on my ballerina tutus. You would have thought we were doing Broadway productions right there in Liberty, Texas! She never complained. Not once. I loved her dearly.

My mother always said that when you have a small family or no family, you get to pick them out for yourself. The Dennison family certainly filled that role, and Elouise and Felton's daughter, Ann, was and is like a true sister to me. Fourteen years older than me, she built my creativity and curiosity through fun and games, sometimes on horseback. I will never forget the day she left for college. I sat in my mother's kindergarten classroom and cried my eyes out, saying, "My bestest friend ever is leaving me." She never really left me, and has always been like my sister as we navigate life.

It was a different time for sure. We didn't know anything about what was politically correct. And we certainly had no concept of privacy. People thought nothing of just "dropping by"—arriving unannounced, just to see what was going on. People casually wandered in and out of each other's homes. These impromptu meetings kept things interesting. Everyone knew everyone and everything about you. If you had visitors from out of town, the news would be covered in the local paper a couple of days later. If you "snuck out" of your house as a teenager to toilet paper the quarterback's front yard, inevitably the neighbor who had insomnia would see the whole thing, and as they poured the first cup of coffee in the morning at Layl's diner, it would be the main topic of conversation.

It was a wonderful life on the surface. Liberty was in the middle of an oil boom; it was an exciting time. Deals were being made, a new country club was built, and fortunes were won and lost overnight. My dad was right in the middle of it all and, by all appearances, everything was fine.

SUDDENLY HE WAS GONE

My dad was haunted with nightmares about his combat experiences in World War II. He would scream from his dreams at night. In retrospect, I'm sure he had post-traumatic stress disorder (PTSD), but people did not understand it at the time. He drank too much. There were horrible arguments that I witnessed and fights between my parents, mainly over money. Eventually, he was prescribed Valium, a powerful tranquilizer.

The medical community at the time did not understand the dangers of Valium. One night the combination of alcohol and the prescription medication killed him. I was thirteen.

Suddenly, he was gone.

A guy who had served with my dad in the Navy showed up from California to attend his funeral. After the ceremony was over and we were all visiting, he told Mother and me why my dad had a scar on his neck. He told us that he was with my dad in the Philippines and that my dad was left on the beach as a casualty. He was stabbed in the throat by a Japanese soldier. The medics were putting him in a body bag when he found his last bit of energy and courage and reached out and said, "Let's give it the old college try." They were able to save his life that day.

My mom and I had never heard that story before. We could not believe it. As strange as it may seem, the men and women who served in World War II were told, "Go back to work or go to college and move on with your lives; leave it behind." Rarely did anyone talk about the atrocities of the war. But many, like my dad, were not able to leave it behind.

"NEVER BE AFRAID TO TALK ABOUT YOUR DAD"

Mother's friends, like mine, tried to get things back to "normal" for us after his death, but they allowed us to grieve. My mother said right off the bat, "Never be afraid to talk about your dad. As long as we talk about him, we will keep him alive in our lives and hearts." We did talk about my dad a lot, and because of it, I remember to use his sharp wit, intellect, and compassion for people every day of my life. He is always with me.

Dottie Warren was not long wounded after being left a

widow at the age of forty-three. She somehow recovered. Dottie was tough, resilient, and independent. Asking for help just wasn't in her DNA. However, she didn't have to ask for help when Dad died in May 1969. The people of Liberty didn't let us down, and supported us with love, advice, and just pure human kindness. Sure, I was terribly sad at times, but I never felt alone. Everyone knew exactly what was going on and helped the best way they could. That sense of community, filled with homespun humor, helped my mom and me to move on.

Mom went on to do great things, enjoy life, and was the best cheerleader I could have ever dreamed of. I naturally became the center of her life. And she wanted me to be the center of everyone's life. I half jumped and she half pushed me onto the drill team, debate teams, student council, National Honor Society, plays, parades, and trail rides. I was in everything and excelled. In fact, if I did not have my picture in the *Liberty Vindicator* newspaper once a week, she would be outraged. I had so many opportunities to perform at an early age in front of amazing crowds and people. I was confident and poised, but along the way I felt that I had to do all of this to please the people who loved me. They counted on me to win. They were all deeply invested in my success. Sometimes I pushed myself so hard to win and be loved—to make the people who adored me proud. After my father died it got even worse. As an only child, I had to please my mom. I was all she had in this world. This put daily pressure on me to add to my list of accomplishments. My mother was caring and loving but a very demanding taskmaster. She believed it was all for my own good, but now I understand that a lot of her worth was tied up in my success. It was tough to live up to such standards. No matter how high I jumped, there was always a new hurdle facing me.

TAMALES IN MY LIFE

I collect tamale stories, so indulge me one here: In Texas, tamales are part of the traditional Mexican celebration of *las posadas*, which commemorates Mary and Joseph's search for shelter before the birth of Jesus. The steamed, husk-wrapped bundles of *masa* (corn dough) and meat are a part of our culture. Throughout the years the labor-intensive process of making tamales became a social event for ranch women. Rhett Rushing, folklorist at San Antonio's Institute of Texan Cultures, said, "By the time the day was over and the tamales were made, the family would be caught up, the arguments resolved, differences aired. It wasn't just about the *masa* and the meat. It was the love and tears."[3]

For me, the significance of tamales dates back to my childhood and my dad's introduction of them to me. Every year my dad would go to Del Rio, on the Texas side of the border with Mexico, to deer hunt with his buddies. To prepare to meet and greet some of the Mexicans in Villa Acuña, on the Mexico side, he would listen to Spanish records before turning in at night in my parents' bedroom in Liberty. He would lie on the bed in the dark, repeating Spanish phrases, and all you could see was the burning ember of his cigarette.

One year he insisted that my mother and I go with him to the deer lease. Not so much to hunt deer, but to meet some of his new friends. I remember driving over to Acuña one evening and coming upon a very modest dwelling. My dad jumped out of the car and knocked on the door, and out came a man with a big smile on his face and a hug for my dad. Dad motioned for us to come in.

Once inside all that was spoken was Spanish. My dad was so excited to be able to practice all he had learned. Mother and I were a bit out of the loop, but felt welcome. They served us a typical Mexican meal of refried beans, rice, and tamales. I had never had a tamale before, but they sure were good!

In 1964, there was only one Hispanic family living in Liberty, and certainly no Mexican restaurants. But that same year after our taste of tamales in Mexico, my dad decided he would ask Mrs. Garcia in Liberty to make tamales for us. Her son, James, delivered them to us, and my dad paid him and gave him a nice tip. This tradition went on until my father's death in 1969. Mother and I had enjoyed the tamales, but never knew that my generous father was also encouraging and helping James.

Like many others, James made the walk up our stepping-stone to our house the day my dad died. With tears in his eyes, he confided in us how much my dad had meant to him because Dad had gone out of his way to treat him with kindness and respect.

And to think, it all started with a dozen tamales.

For years after his death, people would tell me stories of acts of kindness Dad did that my mother and I never knew about. Some were simple; some were pretty big efforts to help people. He never asked for any credit or told us about his desire to help people. Today, I am still in awe of his profound acts of kindness in that little East Texas town.

LIVING BEYOND OUR MEANS

My mother always lived above her means. It was important to her to appear affluent. She bought me lavish gifts and ran up big bills at Neiman Marcus and other Houston department stores. She accepted money from her parents, which made my dad angry because she was spending too much. And it embarrassed him that she was always trying to appear more upper class than we really were.

I began to realize that our financial resources were limited and that my mom was not very good about managing money. I took over my own finances at fourteen years old. I got a monthly support check from the Veterans Administration and Social Security. I opened my own checking and savings accounts. I got a job doing engraving in a jewelry store. Mother was always wanting to buy me something, and I was usually able to slow her down.

My father had taken a partial interest in some of the land he surveyed instead of charging the owners fees. When my mom needed extra money, she would sell a piece of land. I did not know about this until I was a senior in high school.

I got an art scholarship to the University of Texas at Austin. Felton Dennison helped pay my sorority dues and loaned me a Jeep to drive back and forth to Austin. I was able to get a job as a teaching assistant in the art department. I got by but just barely.

One Saturday morning, Dottie drove to Austin accompanied by one of her friends, who was driving his big shiny Rolls-Royce. She waltzed into the University of Texas Pi Beta Phi sorority house with a gift box in hand. I heard a page go through the house, and I was summoned to the front foyer. When I got downstairs I was delighted to see my mother, until I looked at the rather large box. I thought, "Oh my, what has she bought for me now?" Imagine my reaction when I opened the box and found a chinchilla coat.

I was devastated by the thought of what it must have cost. I tried to maintain my composure and not embarrass her in front of the crowd that had assembled. Some forty years later I still have that coat. I have taken excellent care of it, but I am always reminded every time I wear it that money doesn't come easy. That day I took total control of her finances. Within a few weeks, when I better understood her financial situation, I realized that I would have to help support her for the rest of her life. She had gone through all the land, was basically broke, and was living on a teacher's salary. And she bought me an expensive coat. I grew up pretty fast.

Here I was struggling with my own finances and yet I was living in a sorority house full of girls from some of the wealthiest families in Texas. Living up to my mother's expectations, the expectations of my sorority sisters, college professors (and not to mention the high goals I set for myself), I had a tough burden to carry. At times, I almost hit the wall. I found myself driven almost to the point of depression, and it required a deep self-examination about who I was, what I wanted to do with my life, and what it was really all about.

I tell these stories, good and bad, because all of my values and ethics come from my family, the Dennisons, and all those wonderful characters from Liberty, Texas. When my instincts kick in, they are the culmination of all of these stories.

COLLEGE AND A ROCKY START ON A CAREER PATH

I had a great time at the University of Texas. I lived two entirely separate lives. As an art major I always dressed in blue jeans and a big floppy T-shirt. When I came back to my sorority house, I changed into much more fashionable attire and lived the Greek life. Many of my Pi Beta Phi sorority sisters at the University of Texas came from the wealthiest families in not just Texas, but the entire South, and I was intimidated by them. After about six months in, I started to feel snubbed by some of the "big-city" girls. They looked down on me as a small-town hick. So, I was determined to show them I was worthy. I took on leadership roles at UT and in Pi Phi. I made top grades and was asked to join several honor societies.

Through my wit and humor, I won them over. I was invited to their lavish debutante balls, and private parties in their family mansions. I learned so much from these people. It was the first time I walked into a home and saw art on the walls by painters who I was studying in my art classes. I got spoiled staying at one friend's home in Highland Park, in Dallas, when I was invited for the Texas–OU football weekends each fall. Servants would wake me in the morning with fresh-squeezed orange juice, and freshly baked homemade biscuits and croissants. We had brunch at the Dallas Country Club and took the bus to the Cotton Bowl to be a part of the pageantry and energy of the big game of rivals. My Pi Phi friends were included in so many events and celebrations that I would not have experienced without their kindness. Many of us are still close friends to this day.

I sat up straight in the saddle, put myself out there, and proved I was competent.

At the University of Texas, I was considered by my creative advertising professor to be one of his top students—one who could land a job at any of the best New York advertising agencies. He thought anyone in the advertising business who was not in New York was a loser. Instead, I chose to take a job at The Richards Group (a smaller, boutique creative agency on a fast track) in Dallas, where my fiancé was in dental school. My UT professor was furious when he learned of my decision. He never spoke to me again. I always wanted to ask him why he was teaching advertising in sleepy old Texas, but I couldn't because we weren't speaking.

I was the second woman at The Richards Group ever hired in the creative department. The catcalls and razzing I had to deal with in those early days make *Mad Men* look pretty tame. The first day on the job, I was shown to my little cubicle and given my first assignment. This went pretty well for a few months, but over time I felt more and more isolated, and the creative muses got harder and harder to call upon. I felt like I was almost brain dead. At the time, I was working on Air Florida mechanicals (the manual way we had to put together ads in those days) that were both tedious and something I was not trained to do in the first place. Life became so miserable that one day, Stan Richards and I came to the same conclusion. It just wasn't working and I needed to move on.

Devastated that I had failed, I couldn't figure out why I had been so successful as a teaching assistant at UT, where I would brainstorm with other students about great ad concepts. I would later come to understand that my personality type doesn't do well at all in isolation.

FINDING A BETTER PLACE TO BE

When I left The Richards Group I only had two weeks' severance pay, and I had to get a job pronto to make ends meet because my husband was still in school. Thankfully, I landed a position at Baylor University Medical Center in Dallas, the largest health-care facility in the Southwest. My role was in media relations, and I thrived. I quickly became accustomed to the drama associated with hospitals. I sat in on a surgery to repair a hand almost completely cut off by a band saw—

the first successful procedure of its kind. I was there in the early days of rapid advancement in heart surgery. I was in and out of the emergency room, and while I never became callous to the blood and gore, I learned how to deal with it like any cowgirl would do. I honed my writing skills, did hundreds of interviews, and made friends with almost everyone.

Within the year, I was promoted to assistant public relations director at the ripe old age of twenty-two. This was 1978. Boone Powell, Sr. was chairman of the Baylor Foundation at the time, and he and I worked on several fund-raising projects together. He took a real interest in me and became my first mentor. Several months later, the director of public relations had to leave due to a troubled pregnancy. Instead of going outside to find a new director, Mr. Powell and my boss tapped me for the role. I couldn't believe the responsibility they gave me, but with their help and the help of a great staff, we achieved some true milestones. Later when I told Mr. Powell that I wanted to get my MBA in marketing, he asked, "Why?" I tried to explain and then he interrupted: "Forget it. You could sell ice to Eskimos."

One early morning I woke up in Dallas to a phone call from the US State Department informing me that Baylor would be receiving a very high-level international political prisoner. They planned to "move in" to my office to help manage the surge of national press reporters. The patient was Benigno Aquino, Jr., who was jailed in the Philippines by Ferdinand Marcos, but was allowed to travel to Dallas to undergo a coronary bypass.

As soon as I could get to the hospital, I went to Mr. Powell's office and told him I was scared I would make a mistake or misstate something. He looked me in the eye and said, "The very fact that you are going to be so cautious makes me know you will not screw this up." I didn't screw it up. And I got a huge boost in my confidence and in myself because of the unconditional faith Mr. Powell had in me that morning. And I learned that I was completely capable of dealing with the press.

I got to spend some time with Senator Aquino while he was recovering. I remember him telling me that he would be assassinated if he went back to the Philippines. I assumed he would seek asylum in the United States. But he did go back in August 1983 and was shot at the Manila International Airport (which now bears his name) while disembarking the China Airlines plane he flew in on. I am still stunned today by his bravery.

LEARNING MORE ABOUT MYSELF

My husband was accepted to the orthodontics residency at Emory University, so off we went to Atlanta. It would be my first time to live outside of Texas. In an interesting twist of fate, I passed up an opportunity to work at a large advertising agency and instead took a job working with Leadership Dynamics, a management consulting practice owned by a couple of Harvard MBAs. They specialized in business consulting, mainly in the areas of leadership development, team building, motivation and strategic planning for Fortune 500 companies. Again, I thrived because it was a people job. They taught me about the Myers-Briggs Type Indicator (MBTI) and how to use it to build more effective management teams. That experience in learning to understand people based on personality type was one of the biggest influences on my future career. Those guys were so smart. The knowledge I gained from them and the case studies I was writing was worth far more than that MBA I wanted.

I learned about the intricacies of the MBTI and the DiSC Model of Behavior and really started to understand my own strengths and weaknesses. I learned that, to be successful, I had to surround myself with people who I could collaborate with, people who would share ideas with me so we could make them better. I remember that when I understood that, it was like a lightbulb going on. Again, at an early age, my career was catapulted because I was realistic about my leadership style and learned to be able to see myself objectively. And I had already learned through painful lessons about my weaknesses.

We saw challenges with personality types come up over and over again in our consulting work with corporate management teams. People tend to be drawn to people who are like-minded. Introverts tend to flock with introverts. Feeling people love to be with other feelers. But allowing teams to be type-heavy one way or another is a recipe for disaster because the teams will consistently be blind to other ways of thinking and doing. The MBTI assesses personalities along four mental functions—sensing, intuition, thinking, and feeling. It also examines four attitudes—extraversion, introversion, judging, and perceiving. The combinations yield sixteen possible personality types. I was hooked and became a lifelong student, champion, and teacher of the intricacies of personality type.

Lessons Learned: The Early Days

- If you can open your heart and treat each person who comes into your life with respect and genuine interest, you will touch people in a way that lifts them up. You will make their day better, and maybe their life better. Each act of kindness will give you the strength to do more tomorrow.

And you will always be delighted when someone surprises you, perhaps years later, and returns the act of kindness or support. My mother always loved the phrase: "Practice random acts of kindness."

- When you are young, test yourself. Try lots of different things. Be completely honest with yourself about what you do well and what you don't. Pour your energy into your strengths. Find others who can shore up your weaknesses and learn that great teams are built this way.

Florence LaDue circa 1912
(Historic Photo Archive/Getty Images)

Chapter 3

FINDING MY OWN POWER—THE
ADVERTISING BUSINESS

You might say that Florence LaDue (born Grace Maud Bensel in 1883) had a difficult childhood. Her mother died from childbirth, and her father, who was a criminal lawyer and later a judge, could not care for her, so he sent her to live with her grandparents, who worked on a Sioux reservation in Minnesota.

In those early days of her life, Florence could be seen alongside her Sioux brothers and sisters riding horses bareback, swimming in the creeks, marveling at the stars, and basically learning the ways of the Sioux.

Her father feared she was becoming too much of a tomboy, and took her back at age twelve to attend school. Although later in life she stressed the importance of education for women, at age seventeen she ran away from home and school to join a Wild West show, where she performed roping stunts and tricks that she had learned on the reserve.

While roping upside down on a horse in Chicago in 1905, she caught the eye of itinerant cowboy Guy Weadick. They soon become a couple, performing for audiences across North America and Europe. They even had a stint on Broadway in

Wyoming Days and did the vaudeville circuits and Wild West shows alongside Will Rogers. LaDue performed solo, but also with her husband.

Less than five feet tall, she could lasso five galloping horses at one time and retired undefeated as World Champion Lady Fancy Roper after performing for thirty-one years! Accounts of those who knew her said she would often say, "Look your best, do your best, and be your best." As tough a competitor as she was, she was elegant and ladylike and always wore a dress or skirt unless she was on horseback.

But Florence knew more than just trick roping. She learned the business of the business she was in. Her husband, Guy, was credited with starting the Calgary Stampede in 1912, but history tells us that she was the businesswoman behind the Calgary Stampede, which today is an annual rodeo, exhibition, and festival. This ten-day event held every July in Calgary, Canada, attracts over 1 million visitors annually. Guy and Florence came to Alberta from the United States to not only start the Calgary Stampede, but also to instill their values, creativity, and eye for talent. Because of her childhood experience on a Sioux reservation, she insisted when they started the Stampede that the First Nations people should be an active part of the exhibition.

As I was writing this chapter of the book, I could only admire what I have learned about Florence. Her tenacity for learning the business she was in inspired me, as I believe it is so important for each of us to get down to the nuts and bolts of how to run a sound, ethical, and profitable business.

Florence was a talented athlete, businesswoman, wife, partner, and cowgirl. When she died in 1951, Guy placed these simple words on her gravestone: "A Real Partner."

After dental school my husband and I returned to Austin,

where he joined an established orthodontic practice. I had wanted to be in a bigger city because I thought moving to Austin was probably a career disaster for me. Back in 1982, Austin was a sleepy, laid-back university town. But I quickly got a job at a local advertising agency—The William Lacy Company. The agency was founded by an early Austin advertising pioneer—Bill Lacy. Bill had a nice big office, with a huge ficus tree in the corner that had two leaves on it—because he chain-smoked all the time, filling the room with a cloud of smoke that left that poor ficus tree barely clinging to life.

In those days, Bill ran the entire company on several yellow pads. He had a pad for expenses and a pad for income. After a few weeks with the company, I went in and asked him to teach me the basics of agency finances. He was thrilled, because no one had ever shown any interest before. He would point out key ratios to watch, profitability targets, people costs, and the all-important process of getting paid—collections. When he saw that I was catching on, he got so excited—sometimes he would have two or even three cigarettes going at the same time. I'm not kidding.

Bill called me his beehive girl because I was always involved in everything, networking and buzzing around. I remember him calling me into his office one day saying that Texas American Bank had a last-minute project and I was going to have to run like a spotted ape to get it done. I did.

The agency was full of characters. The production manager was an old Army drill sergeant. I'll never forget that when you went into his production room, the carpet actually stuck to your feet because of years and years of spray mount residue on the floor. The biggest innovation of the day was slide shows. We had a guy who produced multi-projector slide shows where images moved and slides appeared in sync with the music. We watched his shows and thought we had seen it all.

Soon after I went to work for The William Lacy Company, one of the partners in the firm, Lee Gaddis, told me he would introduce me to my first account, so we drove out to the Texas Hill Country and I met Murry Burnham, founder of the famous Burnham Brothers Coyote Calls. His store was full of archery equipment, traps, knives, and gun safes. But Murry's real claim to fame was his homemade coyote calls. He was shrewd enough to have become the most famous coyote caller in the country, a fact that he promoted prominently in his annual print catalog. Coyote callers all over the world waited with bated breath each fall for the catalog to arrive in the mail. My job was to update the last year's catalog with new products and get it printed. Some of the products were pretty strange, especially something called "Buck Magnet." I read the label and the main ingredient was doe urine!

Murry always had a wild look in his eye and sometimes he just disappeared for days. I guess he was calling coyotes.

I was horrified by the whole thing. I was even more horrified when I learned that Murry kept a collection of live rattlesnakes in the storefront window. I was a magna cum laude graduate of the University of Texas, and here I was hawking doe urine to hillbillies. But I pulled my cowgirl boots on and we got 'er done! Guess what Murry's son was named? Hunter, of course.

I had some other less colorful clients and I learned how to work with them all. I learned that it was critical to build trust at the highest levels of clients' organizations as was possible. It takes time, but if you can build real trust, it can last for a lifetime. When I could build relationships at the upper-management levels, then our direct clients that we worked with on a day-to-day basis could relax a bit because they were not ultimately responsible for our success or failure.

LEARNING TO BRAINSTORM

By this time, I had hit my stride at the agency and was really learning to be a player in the advertising business. Doyle Fellers, president of the firm, taught me how to make ideas—how to brainstorm. Doyle was a talented presenter and spoke professionally all over the country. His favorite problem-solving technique was what he called "Brown Paper Sessions." He would cover the conference room walls with butcher paper, almost from floor to ceiling, using every available surface. He would invite clients in and we would help them define their goals, find market opportunities, and solve problems for their companies. Doyle could have been a great snake oil salesman, because he was fearless. He'd walk into the room—with maybe twenty people attending—stare at the blank walls, and say, "This is going to be so much fun!" He would start to ask questions, probe, write, and laugh. People loved it.

Doyle could read the crowd. When he would uncover an idea that our firm could help execute, he would probe for how much support it had. If he found that the leadership was interested in a topic, he'd walk away and come back to it later and set it up to be their idea. Doyle taught me to smell opportunity—something I can still do to this day.

I quickly learned how to be an active player. I used my Myers-Briggs training and would chime in to pull ideas out of the introverts and try to throttle back the extroverts. I would take an idea and present it from a thinking perspective, and then again from an intuitive perspective. It forced people to step out of their comfort zone and think about different perspectives. Every idea was written down, acknowledged, valued.

What was so special about his approach was that the participants were almost all from our client's organization—people who worked together every day. But they typically worked in silos, in their own departments. No one had ever asked for their opinions before. They had never had an opportunity to brainstorm, to collaborate and talk openly about problems and opportunities. They never thought much about the big picture. They riffed off of each other's ideas and left laughing, energized, and thinking that Doyle was brilliant. We would come out of those sessions with tons of work and bigger budgets. When it was done the room looked like the workshop in the movie *A Beautiful Mind*. We would always go have cocktails afterward and do a postmortem.

I *worked* my network and developed a few opportunities with some of the people I had known at Baylor in Dallas. A few of my connections had become managers at smaller regional hospitals and they needed marketing help. We did some wonderful campaigns and I hit it off with the marketing people, the physicians, and management teams. Before long I had five hospital accounts—in mid-market Texas: Abilene, Midland, Gonzales, Sherman, and Temple.

DIVORCE. NEW LOVE. NEW FAMILY.

When I married my first husband I was young, naïve, in love, and I did not think it through. But after my daughter, Rebecca, was born, it was clear we had conflicting agendas. He adamantly opposed my pursuing and continuing my business career. I was adamantly dedicated to having a successful career and family. This was one of those times when you confront your principles and learn how committed you are to them. I will not bore you with the details, but we decided to divorce and go our separate ways. So, for all of you single moms out there, I have walked in your shoes.

I learned so much during my first years in the advertising business. I proved that I could help produce great work. My experiences in art school, with The Richards Group, with Baylor Medical Center and my Leadership Dynamics buddies gave me the insight and tools I needed to define problems and then guide creative teams to wonderful solutions. This is where I found my passion for the business. It all suddenly *came together* for me. This was when I fell in love with the advertising business. Nothing was more exciting than to see smart people working as a team and do work that none of us could have accomplished individually. I loved the creative process and still do to this day.

Along the way, I ended up in a relationship with Lee Gaddis, one of the partners at the agency. We had been good friends and enjoyed working together for years. But one day, something clicked, and before long, we were married. It is an interesting relationship because you could not find two people who are more different. I am an extrovert; he is an introvert. I'm big picture; he sweats the details. We learned that those differences enabled us to support each other in powerful ways. Lee had two boys from a previous marriage: Ben, who was older than Rebecca, and Sam, who was younger. Of course this complicated things, but we worked through them day by day, step by step.

Before we married, Lee warned me that when you are falling in love, you have on rose-colored glasses. He said, "The reality of our lives will be their dirty little socks and peanut butter and jelly sandwiches smeared on the floor of the car." I accepted the challenge.

But it was a tough time for all of us, learning to bring a very young family together. We put our heads down and the kids thrived. We did amazing things with them, but our favorite thing to do was to load everyone up on Friday afternoons and head to South Texas to the little town of Cotulla. Lee's family is an old respected ranching family. These South Texas people were stoic compared to the gregarious folks I grew up with in East Texas. They were largely of German ancestry and firmly believed that the less said the better. Gabby people were frowned upon. Talk about tough!

To give you a sense of who they were, my husband's great-grandfather, George Washington Maltsberger, was born six years before the Alamo fell. At fourteen years old, he left the farm he grew up on in Tennessee to pursue a colorful life as an adventurer, pioneer, Indian fighter, soldier, and stockman. He led one of the migrations of Mormons to Utah as a young man. When he decided to leave Tennessee and move to Texas, he blazed the trail riding two days ahead of his family to scout the best route. His father, accompanied by George's fiancée, Roxana Allen, followed behind in their covered wagon.

Each night George would pick a place to camp, and he would carve a single heart on a tree to mark the spot. Then Roxana, who was an adventurous and skilled trail leader in her own right, would lead their band to the campsite a few days later. She would follow the hearts that George had left her, marking them with a second heart, along with a bar to connect them, so George would know how far she had proceeded in case she failed to appear at camp—which she never did. It was in this fashion that they ultimately made their way safely to San Antonio, got married, and started raising cattle, using the Double Heart brand that had brought them together in love, and in life.

Lee's dad, Harry Gaddis, was a pharmacist and a bank director as well as a working rancher. Harry had passed away several years before we married, but his mother, Isabel Maltsberger Gaddis, was still very active and we became great friends. She was an expert horse trainer in her younger years, was a teacher, writer, and a folklorist of the vaqueros of the Texas brush country.

She taught me how to hunt for Indian arrowheads on the ranch, and I developed an almost mystical sense when I was close to finding one. The kids loved visiting the ranch and riding around in a big hunting rig, shooting guns, chasing jackrabbits at forty miles an hour across salt flats, and hearing spooky ranch stories over a campfire at night. I make a mean bananas Foster on an open campfire, straight from a recipe I learned as a girl from a waiter at the famous Brennan's restaurant in New Orleans.

Another tamale story: We were spending one Christmas in South Texas. My husband went over to a little store that had a reputation of having the best tamales in the county. He was surprised to find the store closed, unheard of on Christmas Eve. He walked around to the back of the store, where the owner lived in a small apartment. He knocked on the door and the owner quickly emerged. "Why is your store closed?" Lee asked. She replied with frustration, "Every year I make tamales and all of these people come and buy them all. So the next year I make more and the people come and buy them all and want more. So I make more and they buy them all. There is just no satisfying them! So I quit."

We did wonderful things with the children. Sunday nights were Mexican food nights, and we would sit at this funny little family-owned restaurant and have "pun-offs." One kid had to start with a pun, and then each had to try to top it. The one who could not summon up a pun ended up being the goat. We taught them to make up a story and then stop about a third of the way through. The next kid had to continue the story, and the third one had to finish it. They really learned to improvise. I exposed them to a few nasty jokes, which were harmless but made them wildly popular with their friends. And they all learned the lost art of the practical joke.

After Isabel passed away, we sold the South Texas ranch and purchased a ranch in the Texas Hill Country, just about an hour northwest of Austin. We registered the Double Heart brand in Burnet County, just as G. W. Maltsberger had done in Bexar County in the 1860s. Our Texas Longhorn cattle proudly wear that same brand today, some 150-plus years later. In fact, you may not know that the term "branding" that we use in advertising today comes from cattle brands.

Today, the Double Heart brand stands for enduring passion, forging new trails, safe passage, and journeys motivated by love. And the Double Heart stands for a legacy of courageous cowgirls who won't take any guff, who face down risk on a daily basis, know how to walk the walk, take care of business and, most importantly, how to survive no matter how great the obstacle or how great the challenge.

The South Texas ranch, my godfather's rice farm, and the Double Heart Ranch have been an important part of my life. I've learned so much by being close to the land. The ranch is very much a working ranch. Our Texas Longhorn cattle are beautiful. The breed comes from cattle brought to America by Spanish missionaries in the early 1500s. Many of the missions failed, and the cattle went wild and survived. Thousands were driven up the trail to Kansas after the Civil War. You have probably seen the movie *Lonesome Dove*. Lee's grandfather was one of those cowboys. By the late 1920s the breed was almost extinct. A heroic effort went into saving the longhorns and they graze at our ranch today as a symbol of Texas pride.

I have lived a life of remarkable contrasts. A few years ago I had the honor to ring the opening bell at the New York Stock Exchange. Later in the day I caught a plane home to Texas and drove out to the ranch. I stopped to pick up groceries and, as I waited in the checkout line, I heard two men talking about stock prices—livestock prices. I asked them if the market was up or down, and they happily reported it was up. So there I was with a foot in two very different stock markets.

CUTTING MY OWN TRAIL

After years of successfully building client relationships, profitable business, and empowered teams, I became frustrated with the overall direction at the agency. We were doing OK work, but I knew there was a better place to be—the intersection between outstanding creative and work that produced specific, tangible results. I had a few teams already doing it, so I was confident that it could be done. But I wanted the entire agency to put a marker down committing to a higher standard.

So with a small band of insurgents, I developed a new business plan to do just that. We focused on the kind of creative work I was doing for my clients. We wrote the proposal, ran all the numbers, and I finally presented it to our president, who went down the hall to his office to read it in detail. Later that afternoon, he came into my office and told me he would not support my plan, that it was too risky and too expensive.

I left the office fuming, humiliated, and perplexed. The next morning, I walked into the office and quit. I proposed a deal so that I could take my hospital clients with me and compensate the agency by paying a percentage of earnings for several years. Doyle knew I had him over a barrel because he knew he could not keep those clients if I left. No one else had the hospital expertise that I did. So he agreed. I learned another powerful lesson: Always negotiate from a position of strength. I felt pretty strong when I walked out of the office that day.

This was in 1989 and the Texas economy was in terrible shape with the savings and loans crisis and many of the banks failing. Real estate wasn't worth the land it was built on. Getting new business was like pulling hens' teeth. I had a $16,000 IRA. In those days you had ninety days to transfer IRA funds into a different bank account, so I used that as a float to hire two employees, rent a small office, and buy a typewriter and some furniture. We did not have a fax machine, but some guys down the hall thought my assistant was cute, so they let us use theirs.

At the time, starting my own company seemed like an extremely risky move. I really believed in what I was doing, and so I leaned on my cowgirl legacy, bet on myself, and made the leap. That doesn't mean I wasn't scared, but as John Wayne once said, "Courage is being scared to death but saddling up anyway." (I did get the money back into the IRA account in just under ninety days and avoided the penalty.)

A few months after I started the company, Lee and I were

having dinner at one of our favorite restaurants. He was goading me as only he can. He said the last thing the world needed was another little advertising agency and asked me what I was going to do to differentiate my business. I started talking about the intersection of creative and results and winning awards. He stopped me in my tracks and called bullshit on me. I had a glass of wine and tried again, only to be shot out of the sky like a dove dropped with a twelve-gauge shotgun. I had another glass of wine and was getting pretty mad. Finally, I burst out, "Damn it! I want to do kick-ass work for clients who want to kick ass!" He got up and grabbed a paper napkin from the bar and wrote down what I said. He handed it to me and said, "That's your business plan." That napkin is framed in our lobby at T3 today, and that unorthodox mission statement has never changed. Our "Kick Ass" mission statement has been a powerful guide in keeping us on one simple but aspirational path.

Our agency, T3, started to grow pretty rapidly. We picked up Prime Cable, selling cable subscriptions in markets as far away as Alaska. We won ESPN's top national campaign for that work the first year. We won two national ADDY Awards in our first few years in business. And our work was making the cash register ring for our clients. This was exactly where I wanted the business to be.

I remember when the Prime Cable marketing team came to our office to interview us about working with them, and I heard the phone ringing a lot more than normal. When they left, I asked my assistant what was going on with all those calls. She smiled and said, "Oh, that was me calling myself. I just wanted the office to seem busy." She was a cowgirl.

BUILDING MY COMPETENCE

Our first real growth at T3 came from me drawing on my health-care contacts. Marketing hospitals was a relatively new game, and very few advertising agencies had any real credentials. By developing increased expertise in this narrow field, I quickly became more powerful by building a competence that very few other people had. And during the rough economy between 1989 and 1991, hospitals were some of the few attainable clients who had sizable budgets.

Gradually my confidence emerged as assertiveness as I realized that I was probably the most knowledgeable person in Texas about marketing hospitals. There were only one or two people in the state who competed with me in this highly specialized field. I made friends with the people at the Texas Medical Association, who referred me all kinds of business. I was often asked to present to different hospital continuing education programs, which I loved because it rapidly grew my network.

We had one client, East Texas Medical Center (ETMC) in Tyler, Texas, whose major competitor, Trinity Mother Frances Hospital, was literally right across the street. If our client opened a women's center, Mother Francis would do the same. If ETMC got a helicopter, Mother Francis would soon have theirs in the air. A well-respected hospital consultant told me, "If Mother Frances put a yellow submarine on the front lawn, ETMC would have theirs out on their lawn in a few days."

We worked our referral network and soon represented a large hospital system in virtually every major market in Texas. I purposefully restricted my client base to Texas, so I could fly out in the morning to see our clients and get back that evening to be with my family. I could have easily grown our business way beyond Texas because of our specialized expertise, but this was the time that I realized I could manage the size and scope of my business to fit my family needs. I did not always make it home for dinner, but rarely missed reading books like *Goodnight Moon* to the sleepy children at bedtime.

THE LIBERATION OF BEING A THINK TANK

When I started T3, I wanted it to be a "marketing think tank," not an advertising agency. That's where the T3 name came from: The Think Tank. We saw a lot of clients trying to solve business problems with advertising when there were better alternatives than just another ad. So we began to build a port-folio of "idea" people not traditionally found in an advertising agency. We brought in architects, psychologists, strategists, and presentation experts—all bringing different points of view to the table. It was an exciting time. Looking back, I see this as a major pivotal point in my life. Defining ourselves as a "mar-keting think tank" was clearly a power play that led to real innovation that was ahead of its time.

Two early examples of think tank solutions are emblazoned in my memory.

The first one is when a couple of guys came to us who owned check cashing stores across Austin. The purpose of these stores was to serve people who simply didn't have tradi-tional bank checking accounts. Most of them couldn't afford the bank fees and were living paycheck to paycheck. Our client's stores were named Money Box. After we put our think tank approach to work, we realized that the customers they were seeking rarely bought or read a newspaper. Many had no automobiles, and didn't listen to the radio. Television was out of reach because it was cost prohibitive. Aha! We put their marketing dollars to work by converting their storefronts into large, dimensional structures depicting twenty-dollar bills emerging from the rooftops. The visibility and personality, plus a refresh of the interiors, gave the stores a reputation of being a reliable and safe place to do transactions. Business took off like hotcakes! Mission accomplished.

The second story is about a company called US Brick. During a new-home building boom in Texas, customers had a choice of brick brands. Most people didn't even know there were brick brands. A brick was a brick. T3's think tank philosophy went into high gear. We hired one of Texas's best mural artists to hand paint their delivery vans to look like giant bricks. He even put sand in the paint to create a brick-like texture. They were like driving billboards all over the state, and we even used them to pull into trade show conferences and display brick samples out of the backs of the vans. This idea earned one of the early National Gold ADDY Awards that I mentioned. Once again, award-winning creative thinking intersected with success for our clients.

Around 1993, a friend from my college days at the University of Texas who was working at Dell Computer Corporation asked us to consult on one of their direct marketing programs. Dell had the same problem that most direct marketers at the time had, a lousy database full of duplicate names and bad addresses. This was way before the sophisticated database programs we enjoy today were available, so most direct marketers cobbled together their lists using a variety of third-party vendors. We really did not have that much data management experience at the time, but we did not mention that to Dell.

We made recommendations for some quick, fairly easy fixes, and we also made some long-term suggestions on consolidating vendors. And, while they did not ask us to do so, we came back with our Trojan horse—some creative ideas for direct mail campaigns that we thought could improve results. They engaged us to address the short-term fixes and to test our creative ideas. The campaigns did well and we started to get more work. A lot more work.

Within just a few months the workload expanded rapidly and got a lot more complex, so I asked my husband, Lee, who had his own marketing consulting company at the time, to come help with strategy. Lee and the guys at Dell hit it off, and I ultimately talked him into joining my company. Over the next year we did hundreds of direct mail projects for Dell. We did lots of off-site planning sessions at our ranch just north of Austin. The Dell teams loved to get out of their cubicles, come to the ranch, and work and play hard. Skeet shooting, beer drinking, card playing, late-night storytelling around the campfire with red wine flowing freely. (No one was allowed to drive home; we literally padlocked the gates.) There were late-night poker games as well!

A quick aside: We had a guy working for us who was a great chef, and he cooked at these events. He also was a frequent winner of the poker games. A few years ago we removed some furniture at the ranch and discovered an ace of spades stuck into a crack on the underside of the card table! We always thought he was a skilled player, but maybe not!

The relationships we developed brought a lot more business. At this point we were really functioning as a think tank. The work we were doing was not something that would come out of a typical ad agency. In 1995, working with Dell's senior marketing managers and Vijay Mahajan, from the University of Texas business school, we created the Dell Marketing Academy—a university-level course designed to teach the unique Dell business model to Dell marketers and salespeople. Dell faced a cultural challenge because they were hiring some of the top MBAs from the best Ivy League schools in the business. But those newcomers were often assigned to work with salespeople who had just graduated from Pflugerville High School a few miles up the road. We helped define the direct sales model and taught it as a core business strategy that everyone could understand. The MBAs all thought they had the answer and it turned out that the Pflugerville guys understood it better. It was a simple idea—go for share, not margin. It took a while for everyone to get on the same page. The classes were taught every other Friday afternoon at a nearby hotel meeting room. The original plan called for the course to last about three months. It went on for two years.

T3's success gave us a lot to celebrate, and since my birthday was April 1, we decided that we would own April Fools' Day in Austin by throwing a huge party and inviting all of our clients, vendors, media representatives, friends, and business associates. Clients would come in from all over Texas. It was a huge affair with big tents, a different theme each year, lots of food and drink, and a big band. One year April 1 fell on a Sunday, so we had a huge brunch complete with a gospel choir. The April Fools' parties put us on the map as a major player in Texas.

Dell asked us to take over production of their small business catalog. We hired about thirty people and had the operation up and running in ninety days. I recall being at a small designer dress shop in the Lower East Side of Manhattan, and on the table was one of our catalogs. It was at that moment that I really understood the magnitude of what we were doing. We were touching almost every small business in the United States every month. It was a huge revenue driver for

Dell. It was a massively complex production with hundreds of products in each catalog, extremely detailed technical specifications, and prices that changed every month. Rail cars arrived at one end of the printing plant with massive rolls of paper for the presses. Tractor trailers departed, fully loaded with catalogs, to all of the major postal distribution centers across America.

In 1996, Dell started selling computers online. Their business simply exploded. A year later, online sales were running at $3 million per day.[4] Now IT managers could look at their monthly catalog to understand the options, and then go online to configure a computer to meet their unique needs twenty-four hours a day, seven days a week, without having to put up with a pushy salesman from Texas.

We watched it all unfold before our eyes. We predicted that the Internet would someday be at the center of all marketing activities. Some clients and staff looked at us like we were crazy. "Well, crazy is as crazy does," said Forrest Gump.

It was all new. There was no one to teach us. So we did the cowgirl thing. We hunkered down and learned it. We adopted cc:Mail, one of the first e-mail platforms. We were the first to learn how to use online sales results to make the print catalog more effective. We were the first to build a configurator in an online ad for Dell so that buyers could price their components in real time. We could even directly code to the Dell site and could change pricing in an online ad on the fly.

Dell had grown to become almost a third of our business, and we knew the danger of having a client portfolio that was out of balance. We knew the risks of pursuing Dell's interactive business. But we jumped on it like a duck on a June bug. For Dell, we were a proven partner, we already had all the assets because of the catalog, and we could see the vision and opportunity to be in on the ground floor of the Internet.

In 2002, we opened an office in Manhattan because we were buying lots of interactive media for Dell. We had to do it because no one in Texas knew squat about purchasing interactive media. There were no big business publishers in Texas. We found a team in New York who were considered experts at the time and hired four of them to run our New York office.

Over the next six years T3's relationship with Dell continued to grow. We were recognized with supplier awards and earned larger opportunities within the organization. We developed a strong sense of trust with our Dell clients. We were never the "lead" agency that did national advertising. We were always in the direct marketing or interactive disciplines, which was a good thing because we watched Dell go through five or six different national ad agencies over the years.

In fact, we gradually achieved more status and respect as the bigger agencies fell by the wayside, and we started doing national campaigns for new product launches. Our last big campaign featured real Dell small business customers. We invited them to New York for a celebration and surprised them with ads running on the big screens in Times Square. They were thrilled! I remember watching those people standing in Times Square taking pictures of themselves up on the big screens.

At this point our Dell business was growing so fast we could barely keep up with it. If we had lunch in the Dell cafeteria, we would come back with more projects. So we knew we had a tiger by the tail. The question was, should we throttle the Dell business back so it did not dominate our T3 business? At this point Dell Computer represented about 50 percent of our income. We simply could not grow the rest of our business as fast as Dell. Plus, we were right in the middle of learning the Internet. We took the risk and hung in there because we were quickly building a unique expertise that very few firms had at the time: digital marketing.

LESSONS FROM A FALL

But things change. Dell was not an easy place to work, and many of our personal contacts moved on. In 2008, Dell brought in a new team of marketing leaders. They made a decision to consolidate Dell's global roster of advertising agencies, which ran into the hundreds, down to two or three big global agencies. It made a lot of sense because the complexity of managing different agencies in different countries was daunting. They hired the holding company WPP to build them a custom global agency focused primarily on Dell.

WPP promised to have it up and running in ninety days. They did not even come close. It was a massive project and the idea was flawed. It was too big, too fast, and most advertising people did not want to work for a single client, especially Dell, who was known for execution, not creativity. The whole thing turned into a complete goat rodeo, probably one of the biggest failures in the history of the advertising business. As the months went by, WPP got desperate and decided to try to make our company their Austin hub because, at the time, we were the only thing not broken. One of the Dell marketing executives came to see us to present the idea. We listened with great interest. The only catch was that we had to agree to sell our company to WPP. They believed they had the financial upper hand because Dell was our biggest client and they did not think we could survive without them.

Here we were in another important negotiation, and we did not have the upper hand financially. But we did have principles. Without discussing it at all, we said no. Actually, what we said was a bit more colorful, but you get the idea. We walked the Dell executive out of the building. No one said a word. We called the staff together a few minutes later and told them we were going to be out at Dell. We told them that we were not sure what would happen, but that we would be 100 percent honest with them and they would always know what we knew. We knew we would have to continue working the Dell business until they could find someone else to do our work. We explained to the staff that we would have to make cuts but that we would help them find new jobs. That was no small task as we were heading for a serious economic depression. There wasn't a dry eye in the house, but everyone understood and respected our position. That day was February 14, 2008. We called it the Saint Valentine's Day Massacre. That cloudy day in February, I was stronger than bear's breath. We told everyone that we would perform at the highest level of professionalism until our last project was done. And we did. And we did help everyone who was displaced find another job.

Ultimately we lost about half of our total annual revenue. WPP named their new agency Enfatico. Within less than a year, the new senior marketing team at Dell was fired. This was happening just as blogs and social media were coming on the scene, and the whole thing became the laughingstock of the industry. The entire project was gradually rolled into other existing WPP agencies.

Sour grapes? Not at all. In fact, it was actually the best thing that ever happened to us. I will always be indebted to Michael Dell for the opportunity he gave us. We learned to embrace change and be decisive, and we became an Internet pioneer because of him.

I love the business, but it is not all roses and bluebirds.

A BLESSING IN DISGUISE

Dell's departure was truly a blessing in disguise. We had several teams working on Dell and then another team that worked on everything else. When Dell left, a few people wanted to break out and form "T3 Interactive" to ride the digital wave. I said no. We had always been one big team, and I knew that we would be stronger together. With Dell gone we were able to pull everyone back into one cohesive team and refocus on the quality of our work. Fortunately, several factors aligned perfectly. First, I was free to travel (Sam, our youngest child, had just gone to college)—and I did. A lot. Second, we had real-world digital marketing credentials that few agencies had at the time. Third, major clients were recognizing that digital was not going away and that they had to figure it out.

Thank goodness I had developed a strong network of business people. I called all of them, and pounded the pavement to try to win new business, and thus save as many jobs at T3 as I possibly could. I was honest with all of my contacts. I told them how much money we were losing and why. I explained that I had some fantastic people who were ready to go to work on a new piece of business. My network came through in a crisis.

I racked up millions of miles and gained Executive Platinum status on American Airlines. Every major corporation in America was struggling to build digital marketing infrastructure. They had all decided that the Internet was not going the way of CB radios, as one of my traditional creative directors quipped. Our Internet prowess, which Dell had bought and paid for, became our Trojan horse.

We put ourselves out there, big-time. We won Chase, we won Marriott, we won Universal, we won Microsoft, we won UPS. We replaced the Dell business in less than a year and, in spite of the loss of revenue, made a nice profit. In fact, knock on wood, T3 has made a profit every year since we began. And we have never borrowed a dime to operate the company; we are totally bootstrapped. That is not easy; it means putting the pedal to the metal on new business, growing existing business, or cutting losses before it is too late. It's usually a combination of all three.

Our work was not only great, in many cases it was breakthrough. We did a very early crowdsourced project for Renaissance Hotels where people shared personal snapshots of their favorite vacations on Renaissance's website. We did an interactive tour of the new, updated rooms at Marriott. We were able to watch how consumers engaged with the site online. For instance, the most watched part of our interactive tour for Marriott's newly redesigned rooms was when we showed a tight shot of the computer connection panel on the desk. The road warriors watched this more than anything else because they wanted to be sure they had the right connectors to get online. This is where the Internet got magical.

We've always had opinions and our clients have always had opinions. Suddenly, through analytics, we knew for a fact that more visitors to the site were more interested in the Internet connection than in the showerhead or the thread count of the sheets. Learnings like that cascaded one upon another, and everything we did started getting smarter and more effective because we could measure everything. My original dream of doing great creative and getting tangible results was now irrefutable.

I was frequently asked to speak at industry conferences, and we began to build a very solid, national reputation. I pinched myself to be sure that it was really true. I had built a very successful, very cool company that was worthy of respect and admiration. It took me a long time to get there. But we had arrived.

WHAT TO DO WHEN THE GOVERNOR CALLS?

In 1997, Texas Governor George W. Bush asked me to join the Lower Colorado River Authority (LCRA) board of directors. The LCRA, a nonprofit public utility that manages water, electric generation, and transmission for much of Central Texas, is the biggest wholesale electric generator in the area and employs more than 1,800. I originally said no, that I did not have the time. But he twisted my arm and I went to interview with the general manager of the LCRA. During the interview I told him, "I can't drive all over Central Texas attending board meetings." He said, "Okay, I'll have a ranger drive you."

So, I did the cowgirl thing. I accepted and served for six years, two as chair of the Water Committee. I was the first woman from Travis County to serve. It was an amazing experience—more valuable than the MBA degree I always wanted. I learned so much, met so many wonderful people, and was able to serve the State of Texas with the integrity Governor Bush expected of me. I even got sued by the city of San Antonio over a water deal that had gone wrong. It was complicated but I believe we did the right thing. I wear that fact as a badge of honor. Sometimes you have to stand your ground.

Many mornings I would walk out my back door at the crack of dawn, and there would be my LCRA ranger in his police car, lights flashing, waiting for me with a hot cup of coffee. Off we would go to La Grange or Bastrop or Marble Falls. In my arms would be the huge packets of information we received to review before each meeting; often there would be three or four huge binders of detailed information. The ranger and I would visit and catch up on family news, and then he'd focus on driving and let me work all the way down and all the way back. I even had a badge; no joke.

FINDING MY SISTERS IN SUCCESS

I have belonged to the Committee of 200 (C200) for over ten years. It is composed of half C-suite corporate women and half entrepreneurs, and the members are highly vetted and have achieved remarkable P&L responsibility and positions of leadership. Most are mothers, community volunteers, and board members and are passionately involved in advancing women in the workforce. C200 members collectively generate more than $1.4 trillion in annual revenues and employ more than 2.5 million people. I recently completed a two-year term as chair of C200, so I have personal relationships with some of the most powerful businesswomen in the world.

However, my first C200 meeting was a bit intimidating. I couldn't believe some of the heavyweights in the room. CEOs of major corporations, wildly successful entrepreneurs, and women who had just plain knocked the glass ceiling down. Before long, I realized they were real women with families, issues, and struggles like my own. After speaking with a few members, I felt like I was home.

One of the first women I met was Ellen Hancock. She had been the most senior woman at IBM and was a true force of nature. She was hard-charging, curious, but also helpful and supportive. A couple of years later, Ellen would attend the opening of our T3 San Francisco office and drove my husband and me at breakneck speed through the backstreets of San Francisco in her Rolls-Royce to a dinner engagement. She was a cowgirl!

A TOE INTO TEXAS POLITICS

I was invited to join the Texas Business Leadership Council in 2003, and within a year was the second woman asked to serve on the Executive Committee. This bipartisan group of corporate CEOs and leading entrepreneurs studies issues that affect the ability of businesses to thrive in Texas—issues like transportation, energy, health care, water, and education.

I arrived at my first meeting of the executive committee exactly on time—at 7:30 a.m. When I walked in, the likes of Herb Kelleher, founder of Southwest Airlines, and other Texas business luminaries were seated around the table. I was surprised the meeting had obviously already started. Herb hollered at me and said, "If you aren't at least ten minutes early, little lady, you are LATE." When I was elected chairman of the group several years later, my first act was moving the meetings from 7:30 to 8:30, which meant that we all had to be there by 8:20. Crazy Texans.

Texas has one of the hottest economies in the world, and I give my colleagues on the Business Leadership Council a lot of credit for helping to make that happen. They have made the state a better place to do business. And they have created amazing opportunities for the people of Texas.

It has been great for me to stay on top of key topics and listen to experts from all over the country talk about potential solutions for challenging issues facing Texas. Learning more and more about how politics works has helped me negotiate and influence for T3. Being part of this group has given me a unique platform to give back to the great state of Texas with my time and commitment to excellence.

BULLS. BEARS. BOSTON.

A few years ago I got a call from one of my C200 colleagues, Kim Bishop. She does executive search and board of director placements. Kim said, "Gay, I have an opportunity you are going to be interested in at Monotype." Monotype is a global company and owns over 20,000 typefaces that they license for everything from the printed page to all of our digital devices, even the displays in our cars. After I met the board members and key members of the Monotype staff in Boston, I knew I would enjoy working with them, collaborating and solving problems. I respected them and the operations of the company. And I was thrilled to learn that all of the pre-meeting documents that I used to struggle with when I was on the LCRA board are now automatically loaded on my iPad. How cool is that?

Today my focus at Monotype is to help the company align with the creative communities and to champion innovation. Life comes full circle. I have always loved typefaces. From the time I was a little girl, I would sit at my desk with pen and ink and practice calligraphy and typefaces. Later, as I studied art direction as part of my art schooling at the University of Texas, I would spend hours learning to draw and "noodle" every popular typeface—including Helvetica and Times Roman.

I have learned more about executive compensation, acquisitions, and the SEC guidelines than I ever dreamed of! The due diligence around the governance of the company and challenges we face as board members has made me a better CEO at T3. It is exciting to be actively involved in growing a dynamic, publicly traded global company.

THE MOST EXHILARATING EXPERIENCE OF MY LIFE

I had another opportunity to say yes. I had the privilege to be invited by then secretary of defense Ashton Carter in 2015 to attend a weeklong behind-the-scenes look at our United States military. Along with a group of about twenty-five other notable leaders from all walks of life, we spent six days from way before dawn until late into the night learning about each branch of the military. It was one of the most awesome, inspiring experiences of my life.

I had the opportunity to fly up and down the East Coast in an Air Force C-17 cargo jet. I toured nuclear submarines, drove a coast guard cutter, dined on an aircraft carrier with the crew, and shot targets with the Army Rangers at Fort Bragg in North Carolina—one of the largest US Army installations in the world. The ranger shooting instructors teased me, saying, "I hope you can at least hit one of the targets with that pistol." What they didn't know is that as a cowgirl, I can handle a gun. I nailed six shots in a row, dead center! Talk about fun! They invited me to come back and shoot with them anytime. Sometimes putting yourself out there just means saying yes.

I came out alive and a much better person.

THE BOARD OF DIRECTORS MEETING IN THE HOT TUB

For many years I have traveled at least a third of the time. Long flights, often delayed. Endless meetings. Hotel after hotel. But when I come home, usually on a Friday night, I almost always drive out to the Double Heart Ranch for our weekly board of directors meeting. My husband and I fix a cocktail and climb into the hot tub and call the meeting to order. We catch each other up, talk about our kids and the challenges and opportunities facing the business, and laugh at all of the funny stuff that happened during the week. And we have made many, many decisions during those meetings. One good thing about the venue is that it has kept our board of directors small—just the two of us, and that has been a good thing.

I tell you a few of these stories to give you some of my perspective so you know where I'm coming from. I've had lots of life experiences both good and bad. Mostly good, I'm glad to say. And I have learned some lessons that may be valuable to you. I learned from my mom to make the most in life with the hand you are dealt. I learned from my first job that I have to collaborate with people. I learned what I was capable of when I stepped into that huge role at Baylor at twenty-two years old. I learned to act on the power of my convictions when I had my business plan rejected and started my own company. I learned to access my true grit when we lost our largest account. And I learned that we each have the power to make things better. I want you to have buckets and buckets of goodwill that translate directly into your personal power.

I invite you all to climb on. Let's ride, cowgirls!

Lessons Learned: The Advertising Business

- I found my place and joy in the creative, collaborative environment of the advertising business. Later, when the time was right, I took a huge leap of faith and risked it all to start my own advertising agency. Find your place. Follow your gut, and when risk is staring you in the face, embrace it. Know that if you don't fail occasionally, you are not trying hard enough.

- Evaluate risk and opportunities as a potential investment. Say no to things with poor potential. But when an amazing opportunity comes along that could change your life and create a huge upside for you and your family, raise your hand. Say YES! Throw yourself into it 100 percent, even if the timing sucks.

Fox Hastings with steer
(National Cowgirl Museum and Hall of Fame, Fort Worth, Texas)

Chapter 4

COWGIRLS ARE RESPONSIBLE FOR THEMSELVES

This is probably my favorite photo of a true cowgirl. Fox Hastings is smiling at the camera while lying in the mud holding the horns of a steer she has just thrown. She is completely owning this moment.

Her family thought she was a little wild and sent her off to a boarding school when she was fourteen. By sixteen, she had run away from the school to join the Irwin Brothers Wild West Show doing trick riding events. She had an uncanny way of knowing who she was and what she was good at in life. She was enthusiastic, strong, and an expert horsewoman. She often competed with men and thrived doing so.

In 1924 in Houston, Texas, Fox made her first appearance as a bulldogger, something women had never done before. It was and is about as dangerous as it gets in rodeo—jumping off of a horse onto the back of a five-hundred-pound steer running as fast as he can, then wrestling the steer to the ground by twisting its horns. She was a huge hit. The crowds loved her. Foghorn Clancy, a flamboyant rodeo announcer, made her the most photographed and interviewed cowgirl of the late twenties. She was a superstar.

She was tough and a true professional. She once suffered a broken rib the day before a show opened, but she went ahead and bulldogged her steer for the next three days of the performance. She had a contract to fulfill and never even thought about letting management down. She took full responsibility because the show had to go on.

"If I can just get my fanny out of the saddle and my feet planted, there's not a steer that can last against me,"[5] she said. She became the inspiration to many young women who previously thought a woman's place was strictly in the home.

Cowgirls are raised to be responsible for themselves. At an early age their parents teach them to be self-reliant and self-assured. They learn to not only take care of themselves, but they also learn the responsibility of taking care of their pets and horses. They don't hesitate to muck a horse stall, or to exercise a horse. They learn how capable they are and approach life with a "can-do" attitude.

SADDLE YOUR OWN HORSE

Connie Reeves taught generations of Texas women how to ride. She was a riding instructor at Camp Waldemar, a girls' summer camp in the Texas Hill Country, for sixty-seven years. She helped over 30,000 girls gain confidence in their riding abilities. Connie told every one of them to "saddle your own horse." That phrase has become legendary Texas lore. It means being able to take care of yourself and survive out on the range or in the corporate boardroom. It speaks of the need for independence, not relying on someone else to do your basic tasks. A cowgirl who saddles her own horse does not leave herself open to criticism from the hired hands. She does what needs to be done. She does it because she is self-reliant and capable. She is competent.

COWGIRLS CAN SEE THEMSELVES CLEARLY

When a cowgirl thinks about what she wants to do with her life, she must be realistic and honest with herself about who she is. She is confident, adventurous, bold, steadfast, and dauntless. She is fearless because she knows what she is good at, and where she needs to improve. She is comfortable in her own skin because she is authentic. Because she is not self-absorbed, she is humble. She is not defensive. She can easily laugh at her shortcomings.

Her ability to stand back and look at herself objectively makes her powerful because it helps her set her course and focus on both strengths and weaknesses. Carl Jung wrote, "The privilege of a lifetime is to become who you truly are."

The ability to see yourself from afar is profound. Cowgirls can do it because they take time to listen to themselves, but with a critical ear. They are unafraid of criticism and, in fact, welcome it. They appreciate criticism because they believe their trainer's only goal is to help improve their skills every day. If a cowgirl is holding the reins too tight, she wants to know it so she can learn how to do it correctly.

The ability to see yourself can be challenging. I had a wonderful creative director who was extremely talented. He pursued a career with T3 and we promoted him and built teams around him. But he struggled with it. One day, he came into my office and resigned. I asked him why, and he said that he loved doing creative work, but managing people was extremely difficult for him. The stress and drama of dealing with people was not what he was good at, and he understood it. He went on to build a small, focused business that has been very successful.

Apple has learned this lesson well. They measure many of their employees based on what they produce, not how many people work for them. One engineer who is super talented at code may be more valuable than one hundred other employees. They have fine-tuned their compensation policies to deal with this important reality. Finding the right ways to help people focus on what they are really good at is something that we work on every day at T3. We try not to impose traditional organization constructs on people but instead enable them to thrive with their own unique truth. If you can see yourself objectively, you can take control of yourself and methodically build your own power.

Think about helping your kids. You have the ability to step back and take a critical view of their strengths, teaching them to build on them, get stronger in and more focused on their natural abilities. Teach them to see themselves. Teach them to be quiet and listen sometimes. Send them off to sit by themselves in a deer blind for the afternoon. As my mother always said when I was confused or in the dumps, "Gay, go have a good talk with yourself."

Understand we can't all be great at everything. I am a big note taker. I write lots of notes in meetings and when I hear someone give a really good speech. But I have never figured out what to do with them. They end up in piles and piles. When I get too many piles I put them in sacks. Then I put the sacks in my car, where they stay too long. And, finally, when I drag them into our ranch house, my husband howls with laughter. One of the reasons is that I do not use a computer. I used to do everything, EVERYTHING, on my BlackBerry.

Now I am totally addicted to my iPad and do EVERYTHING on it. So transcribing all of those handwritten notes is just too much trouble. I type so much that I just had carpal tunnel surgery on both of my hands!

I have never been able to remember my passwords either. They are probably on one of those little notes in a sack in the closet at the ranch.

BE AUTHENTICALLY YOU

Penry Price, a Google executive, once told us he had one word to describe T3: authentic. I was amazed and humbled by his comment. There is nothing more important than being who you are and walking the walk.

Cowgirls are authentic. They don't try to be something they are not. They know who they are and how to stand tall. They don't pretend. Around the barn she wears rubber muck boots most of the time, riding pants, and a work shirt. She is comfortable because it is a practical outfit. When she gallops into the rodeo arena wearing her show costume, with glitter and sparkles flashing from the spotlights, and a big white hat, she is just as comfortable.

Cowgirls have a sense of where they fit into the world. They make choices about what to do based on that sense, which is based on long-standing values and ethics that are learned at an early age. Cowgirls do not conform to peer pressure. They only conform to their own gut instincts.

What if you have not had parents or role models cheering you on? What if you have not had a chance to develop cowgirl instincts and values? If you put forth the effort in the classroom or in an early job—you can develop teachers or bosses who will "pump up your tires." This was an old saying my mom brought to Texas from Missouri, and it always rings true.

I have a longtime client who is authentically a real rascal. He has hired me five times as he went from company to company. He is a guy who takes chances. He never plays by the rules. He asks for more out of people and gets more out of you than you thought you had. He loves fast cars and racing. He is fiercely competitive and has an unyielding desire to win. That is why people hire him and why I love him. He is an authentic rascal.

Being authentic means that there are some things you have to do yourself. I have flown across the country to have a private one-on-one conversation with a client about a personnel issue that needed to be handled delicately. I was the only one who could have been as candid about an abusive person on his team who needed to go. We dealt with it over lunch and I was back home for dinner that evening. He resolved the issue the next morning, and we both gained more respect for each other.

No job is too small or too big. Recently, I found myself "shoveling" mouse poop out of some shelves at our ranch. A cowgirl doesn't flinch; she just does what needs to be done because she is authentic.

IT IS ABOUT BOTH DREAMS AND REALITY

Cowgirls learn a lot about life. They are taught about the power of dreams. Dreams give you the power to escape the restraints of reality. With dreams you are free to imagine, roam the earth, fly by the stars. Dreams are about what can be. They are powerful things.

Reality is something entirely different. Reality is understanding who and where you are. It requires you to be totally honest with yourself—to confront the good and bad head-on, with no hesitation or apology. Reality is about the simple facts. It is where you are. You have to look at yourself objectively to do this. It is almost an out-of-body experience, like looking at yourself from afar.

After my dad died and I began to understand how tenuous our financial situation was, I was forced to deal with my mom's aspirational dreams for me and the stark reality of how few resources we really had. My mom never really dealt with it, so I had to. I had no choice; I garnered up the strength and did it. And I kept doing it and it has served me well. I have achieved so many dreams and found real financial success. But the lessons have been tough.

Cowgirls understand. They know how to make magic. They know that when you go through the mental process of combining dreams with reality, you begin to see a road map of what you need to do to achieve your dreams. Dream big, and then be realistic, tenacious, and steadfast in taking the steps to make them come true. *Cowgirls are well grounded.* They understand how to make dreams come true.

MEET PEOPLE WHERE THEY ARE

My dad always taught me to meet people "where they are." What he meant is that it is an art to size people up quickly and be able to almost instinctively greet and interact with them in a way that is meaningful to them and puts them at ease.

My dad worked with some of the most powerful, richest men in the Texas oil business. He also worked with poor, uneducated day laborers who helped him pull surveying measuring lines through the steamy East Texas thickets. He was totally comfortable with people on either end of the spectrum because he respected them all. He always felt it was *his* responsibility to find a way to actually connect with each person he met. My dad taught me as a little girl how to relate to people. He was the master at it. He told me whether you are serving homeless people at the Salvation Army or attending a state dinner at the White House, you need to make people comfortable—to meet them where they are.

One of the characters in Liberty, Texas, was Dewitt Curtis. This was in the early 1970s when Dewitt would put on his wool World War I uniform (in the beastly East Texas summer heat) and walk to the courthouse lawn. He would climb halfway up the front steps and would pull an imaginary violin out of an imaginary case and begin to play it. He would sway with the music, closing his eyes as he heard the sounds that only he could hear.

Brad Pickett was the bank president and one of the county's most respected attorneys. Brad was well known as a straight shooter and was brilliant in the courtroom. When court would recess for lunch, Brad would walk down the front steps and if Dewitt was playing his violin, Brad would stand beside him and pick up his own imaginary violin and begin to play with Dewitt. It was an amazing thing to see because they played together, each hearing the same music that was, or was not, there. Many afternoons Brad returned to the courtroom soaked in sweat and without any lunch. But he was universally loved and respected all over East Texas because he was willing to meet Dewitt where he was. And what beautiful music they played together!

IT IS MY RESPONSIBILITY TO CONNECT

I have had many opportunities to meet people around the world. Each time I meet someone new, I follow my dad's lesson that it is *my* responsibility to actually connect. I own it. A few examples:

I spoke to college students at a university in Beijing, China, about opportunities they might have in the business world. They wanted to share their dreams with me.

I was in a Maasai village in Africa with our guides, Kuseyo and Tuleto. They took us into a mud hut to meet an old woman, the village matriarch. She told us that she had heard that in America people were taking hearts out of dead people and putting them into living people. She asked if it was true. I said yes.

I accepted an award for family-friendly policies at work from then-president of the United States Bill Clinton in the Rose Garden. When I met him I felt like he had this strange ability to see into your soul, which was actually a little disarming.

I have met with some of the most powerful men in the business world. Of course, Texans, but also many leaders of Fortune 100 companies. I am usually humble and polite, but always hold my own, and am not afraid to challenge their thinking.

Last year I was in the galley of a Navy ship talking to a seaman. He told me about how he lost his college hockey scholarship because of a sports injury and ended up in the Navy. I made him comfortable enough that he told me that when he got off work that day he was getting married, going to quit smoking, and buying a new car. I said, "Sounds like a big day!" He left with a big grin.

In Liberty, the only people who were not at the football game on Friday nights were in jail. I can't tell you how many times I have amazed my male colleagues, clients, and friends or fellow travelers at the Admirals Club with my view about the finer points of the game. The guys are always a bit shocked at my ability to talk detailed football strategy, so it is a great way for me to connect quickly to something they genuinely care about.

Being able to quickly relate to people has helped me build solid relationships with my clients. Often we live and work halfway across the country from each other, so when we do have an opportunity to visit, I try to understand what is going on in their careers, their personal lives, and about their dreams and aspirations. If I can do that, we build a special bond. And when I'm on the phone with them months later, I make a point to remember the details they shared with me so I can ask about their daughter or their dog or that promotion. They know I am really interested in them and care about them.

Slow down, reach out, find a quick way to relate. Be authentic and you win power. If this is not intuitive for you, then simply stop talking and listen. There is nothing more tiresome than a person who waxes on and on about themselves. My mother-in-law, the quintessential cowgirl Isabel Gaddis, called them "the unimpeachable source."

Connecting with others is a skill you should teach to your children or nieces and nephews as early in life as possible. My granddaughter is just learning to speak, but she already knows how to make a toast. When she meets someone new, she wants them to have a glass and clink it with hers and make a toast. She then claps her hands and belly laughs.

When I was visiting Botswana I asked one of the guides

about his opinion of which animals were the smartest. He avoided answering for a while, but then he told me I was thinking about it in the wrong way. He said that every animal is clever in its own way. A termite is just as clever as an elephant. Each species has found a way to survive.

It is the same with people. No one has the corner on the truth. Some people have more education. Some have more real-world experience. Some come from wealthy families. Some are poor. Some are not as intelligent. Some are physically challenged, while others are gifted athletes. But by trying to meet people where they are, we show respect to the different talents each individual brings. Watch, observe, connect.

Think about it this way: Each person you meet has a piece to your life's puzzle. When you meet people where they are and really connect, you find that next missing piece that brings you closer to assembling the puzzle of your life.

COWGIRLS ARE RAISED WITH HIGH EXPECTATIONS

Cowgirls are raised by parents with high expectations. They know that their fathers especially expect much of them. Wise fathers understand that girls need to be tough, capable, and strong to thrive in the world, and most try to instill power in their girls. Everyone does not have a great father or role model. I understand that. I was lucky, because after my father died, Felton Dennison stepped in and was an inspiration for me. Later in my life, Boone Powell became a valuable mentor.

Researcher Susan R. Madsen of Utah Valley University did a study of women leaders in China and the United Arab Emirates about their paths to leadership. "Every single one of them talked about finding their voices and their confidence at dinner-table conversations with their families. Their parents talked about politics, about what was happening in the community, and when the women had something to say, their parents didn't hush them," Madsen said. "Every woman I spoke to said her father would bring home books for her to read when he traveled."[6]

Some of my fondest memories were train trips I took from Houston to Saint Louis to attend baseball games, including the 1964 World Series, as a young girl. In the late 1950s and early 1960s, this was a first-class experience. Dolled up in clothes that my mother and I bought at Neiman Marcus, I was escorted to the dining car by my gregarious and witty father. He was always dressed in a stylish suit, with a silk tie and a pocket scarf. He was one sharply dressed man when he traveled.

When seated in the dining car, it was so lovely. Crisp, starched white tablecloths and napkins. Special silverware and china boasting the train's logos. The service was impeccable, and I liked ordering things I had never tasted before, like caviar and beef Wellington. My father would order his favorite cocktails and we would have a nice conversation. Without exception, other passengers would walk by and say, "What a well-dressed and well-mannered young lady." I would beam and my dad would invite them to have a cocktail with us, as he blew smoke rings from a nice cigar. My dad always insisted that I must act grown-up, have a mature conversation, and not act like a silly child. I still remember the stimulating conversations we had with our fellow passengers.

Two of my C200 friends are CEOs of major companies. They also happen to be sisters. Coincidence? No, because they grew up in a household, and with a father, who expected them to plan and budget their lives like a business person. I have loved getting to know Denise Morrison, CEO of Campbell Soup Company, and Maggie Wilderotter, former CEO of Frontier Communications, and to hear the stories of how they started what would be highly successful business careers when they were children.

First of all, at the beginning of each new year, Maggie and Denise were expected to set their personal goals, plan how to achieve them, and provide a budget for all of their projects and objectives. They presented their plans to their dad, and had to negotiate their positions and debate what would be funded or not. They were encouraged to dream big, and that with wise planning, strategies, and plain hard work, they could achieve anything that they aspired to do. Their dad also took them to his office on a regular basis and taught them his business skills, ethics, and techniques for success.

I am just in awe of this story. Was it in their DNA to be successful, or was it through example and careful training from an early age? I have to believe the truth is in the middle. We don't all share the knowledge and wisdom we have learned in our business life with our children very effectively, if at all. Children who are exposed to business lessons and business people early in their lives will have a huge leg up as they start their own careers.

Look back a couple of generations and you'll see that the children grew up in the middle of the family business on farms, ranches, and small businesses. They learned the lessons as they saw life play out in front of them. Today, we get in our cars in the morning and return at night, and far too many of our children hear nothing about what goes on in between.

RIDE HIGH IN THE SADDLE

A cowgirl rides high in her saddle. That means she sits up straight and moves in fluid motion with her horse. Her control of her horse is almost invisible. She is confident. She and her horse understand each other, and respect each other.

How we present ourselves says a lot about our power. I'm a self-confessed fashionista. This comes from shopping at Neiman Marcus and Sakowitz in Houston with my mom when I was little, and having a grandmother who had impeccable taste and could sew like an expert tailor. I always get compliments on my outfits, unless I'm at the ranch; then all bets are off.

Your hair, skin, nails, and overall appearance should be as good as you can make them. Your posture, your gestures, and your mannerisms are the body language that make up your sense of style and how people perceive you. Are you confident, or are you just one of the crowd and not noticed?

One of our most senior client engagement directors has spent the majority of her career at T3. I was walking by one of our think tank rooms and she was leading a team meeting in jeans, a white t-shirt, and flip-flops—totally in control. It was totally her.

Please don't think that I am suggesting you obsess over your looks. I just mean to do the best you can, knowing that time and resources can be your enemy. But take it from our cowgirl heroines, who were "puttin' on the dog" when they stepped into the arena. Just think of yourself stepping into your own arena when you march into the office each day.

For some people, putting themselves together comes easily. But for others, it is really tough and they struggle with how they look, what they look good in, and how to put together a fabulous appearance.

So, this is one time I would say call in the experts. There are wonderful professional stylists, and many stores have people who are trained to do this as well. When I was growing T3 and had young children at home, I hired a very talented personal shopper. She shopped twice a year for me, dressed me head to toe, took pictures of what outfits went together, and hauled off outdated clothes to keep my closet halfway organized. It was a huge help. She saved me tons of money but more importantly, she saved me a huge amount of time—time that I spent with our kids, and building the business and my personal power.

Perhaps you have a friend or family member who has a great sense of style and can critique your look and help you begin to put it all together. The real secret is being able to pull things from a variety of stores and price levels. Expensive clothing is not always necessary. My wardrobe consists of shoes from Payless, designer dresses from Saks, tank tops from Walmart, and vintage jewelry from thrift shops. A nice pair of sunglasses will get you compliments.

I once had a client tell me she was coached to dress in plain clothes—more like a man, and to quit wearing perfume to meetings. I say hogwash—you don't want to be outrageous, but wear what makes you feel confident and powerful. I have been asked many times, if I had to splurge on one item, what would it be? The answer is simple. I would splurge on a killer designer handbag. Why? Because you carry it every day, and they literally hold up better because of the quality and craftsmanship. It makes a statement about you.

Many years ago we hired a financial planner to help us with some insurance issues and be sure we had money for our kids' college education. This guy asked my husband, "Do you have any idea how much money Mrs. Gaddis spends on clothing a month?" I quickly showed him the door.

I knew a powerful, well-to-do woman from an old Texas ranching family. She dressed for the ranch in blue jeans and wore elegant gowns to social events. But no matter what she was wearing she always had a buzzard feather in her hair. She did it all her life. It was a very effective yet simple power play. She was anything but ordinary. She always looked fabulous.

So what is it going to be? A fringed jacket or sequined bustier? Maybe neither one—although on occasion I have worn both, but not at the same time! Just be you.

BUILDING YOUR BRAND

We have a picture of my mother-in-law as a young woman. She was traveling on a ship from New Orleans to New York on her way to attend Columbia University. In the photograph she is posing with other travelers who are all dressed in formal attire getting ready for dinner. But she is wearing a fancy cowgirl outfit—complete with custom boots, a big hat, and a silk bandana tied around her neck. I have looked at that picture of her for many years, wondering why she chose that outfit.

I recently have come to understand. Isabel did not want to blend into the crowd. She wanted to stand out—so she could experience everything the trip offered. And, looking at the smile on her face, I'm sure she stole the show—something she did all her life. We were kindred spirits.

Clothes are just one way to project power. One of the most powerful things I ever did for the T3 brand was to move our office into the Pope-Watson mansion on Rio Grande Street in Austin. It is a gorgeous Greek Revival home built in 1905 with massive white columns supporting a huge, inviting porch. You walk up the steps to the front porch, past the columns, through a hand-carved front door, into a reception room graced on both sides with rooms decorated with fabulous wood carvings done by Peter Mansbendel, a famous Swiss wood-carver, and it just touches you. It tangibly represented who we were and who we wanted to become with grace, dignity, and a long, rich history. The stature and symbolism of that fabulous home defined us, our values, and our desire to succeed. There was also a humorous side to the stately home that looked very much like the Texas Governor's Mansion. The movie *The Best Little Whorehouse in Texas* was shot there, and I would grin sometimes and do a little "sidestep" dance on the front porch just like the Texas governor in the movie. Pretty darn funny for an advertising agency.

We leased the Pope-Watson mansion for a few years and then had an opportunity to buy it. It was a complex, emotional situation with the sellers. We were back and forth with attorneys trying to make the deal. One night, Lee and I were in New York and had just had a wonderful meal at the Gotham Bar and Grill. We had just gone to bed, when the phone rang. It was our attorney saying he had a signed contract but he needed it returned immediately because one of the owners was in very bad health. I told him to fax the contract to the hotel.

I got up and rode the elevator into the lobby of the Plaza Hotel. I walked across that beautiful room dressed in nothing but my mink coat and stilettos. I signed the contract, and as I rode back up to our room, I thought I had reached the pinnacle of success. Buying the Pope-Watson mansion was one of the best, most powerful decisions I ever made.

When I worked for Stan Richards in Dallas at The Richards Group, Stan was fiercely protective of his brand. He stood for creative excellence and would not allow anything, and I mean anything, to go out the door without his approval. It drove the staff crazy and created all kinds of bottlenecks. He was never very good at explaining why he did not like something. But he was fanatical, and he built a legendary, national reputation for creative excellence that lives on to this day.

Your brand is you, what you say, your staff, your office, every document you produce, every presentation you make, and every product you create. Set your standards high and fiercely defend them.

Our son wears a long-sleeved white shirt with rolled-up sleeves, blue jeans, and designer shoes with loudly colored socks every day and pretty much everywhere he goes. He was in a presentation in Washington, DC, recently where everyone else in the meeting was dressed in suits, but he wore his regular uniform and won the business. His unique brand works for him.

TAKE RESPONSIBILITY FOR GETTING FEEDBACK

I graduated magna cum laude only one point away from summa cum laude, because the only C I made while at the University of Texas was in a drawing class. This was fairly early on in my college career. I went to my professor to protest and he said, "Why haven't you been in my office every week trying to figure out how to do better?" I learned the hard way to speak up early if things were not going my way. It was a lesson I never forgot.

Think about the way you receive feedback. Do you seek it out or sit back and wait for it? Are you open to it or do you try to avoid it? People with an open mind-set listen with a focus on improving and learning. Open people look for ways to learn to welcome feedback, including criticism.

In the business world, getting constructive feedback can be a real challenge. If you are in an organization that provides regular constructive feedback, congratulations. But my experience is that most companies are terrible at this, and too many still rely on the awkward ritual of annual employee reviews, which is about as useful as pounding sand in a rat hole. Both sides usually leave these events more confused.

Shelley Correll and Caroline Simard of Stanford University did a research project that "shows that women are systematically less likely to receive specific feedback tied to outcomes, both when they receive praise and when the feedback is developmental. In other words, men are offered a clearer picture of what they are doing well and more specific guidance of what is needed to get to the next level."[7]

Feedback for women tends to be vague and focused more on communication style. When you do receive feedback, be sure to ask questions so that you get information about how you are impacting specific business outcomes. Do not settle for comments like, "You have done a great job."

Speaking with some female university students, one told me that she gave a presentation with three other female students in a class. Afterward, at the critique, they were told they looked good together when they presented. What? She and I were both exasperated that there was not more specific feedback about their content and their ideas. *Cowgirls continue to ask questions until they get useful answers.*

ROUND UP YOUR ROUGH RIDERS

Who is your coach? Who is your trainer? If the answer is always "my boss" you are going to come up short. My advice to you is to read this book and then go about building your own feedback system. Do not wait for someone to do it for you. Start a small group of people who will tell you the truth, and ask for their feedback. Think of this group of trusted souls as your "Rough Riders." They are there to give you insights to make you more powerful. Who else is going to tell you if you are not speaking with enough authority? Who else will challenge your logic? How are you going to improve if you don't understand your strengths and weaknesses?

You reciprocate by being a Rough Rider for each other. Think about the power of this. Think about what an impact it could make on your life and career. Think about having three or four trusted people who will give you candid feedback every day—positive and negative. Team up with your Rough Riders and build on some of the ideas in the section of the book entitled "The Cowgirl Power Toolkit."

Try the Rough Rider idea. You will be amazed what it can do for you. And, I promise, you'll have fun and kick some ass.

DON'T DALLY AROUND—BE DECISIVE

Make decisions quickly and move on. Perhaps the deadliest sin in our businesses is to allow ourselves to agonize over decisions for weeks and months. For example, in our sixteen-year relationship with Dell, the mantra was to get things 80 percent right and execute fast before the market dynamics changed. In those days, prices of computers were falling rapidly. Being at the wrong price point in a monthly catalog could spell disaster. If you wait to get that last 20 percent perfect, you set yourself up to lose. Big-time.

Do what you can do and then go. Always default toward action. You can iterate, improve, tomorrow. What you get done today is what counts. On this point, you can actually see iteration on your mobile phone as the software companies issue update after update. They should stop calling them updates and call them evolutions.

I have seen people pause and freeze in business situations. For example, in my business, the one fatal error is to hold on to overhead when you know your revenue is coming down. We sometimes hope that we can reel in that new piece of business to cover for a loss. If you are lucky, that can happen, but you cannot count on it. My position has always been to cut your losses fast. Carefully and precisely, but fast. You can always rebuild when that next piece of business is signed, sealed, and delivered.

One time, in order to cut overhead, I was going over all of our "nice but not necessary" expenses with my CFO. One item stood out. It was "Candy Friday." Candy Friday was a much-loved tradition where at 10 a.m. every Friday, the bell would ring and bowls of candy magically appeared in the company café. Everyone would stream from their offices, pick out one or two of their favorite treats (some filled up paper cups) while laughing and visiting with their co-workers. I thought, well, we can certainly do without that. Besides, all that candy was bad for people anyway. So I cut it out to economize. No big deal, right?

The first Friday that the candy bowls disappeared was quite devastating. You would have thought I had shot someone's dog in front of our office building. People were outraged! It was at that moment that I realized Candy Friday had become a part of our culture, an icon of our camaraderie and team spirit. It was that special moment each Friday where we began to celebrate the week, exchanged laughs with our team, and got ready for the weekend. The candy was back by the next Friday. I found other ways to cut the budget. So, sometimes a bad decision has to be reversed. Do it as quickly as you can to mitigate the damage. People will forgive and forget.

Women get hung up on perfectionism because they were taught to be more poised and polite, and to make better grades in school than those rowdy boys. Girls were cleaner, more buttoned up, and not as loud. That worked great in the structured school environment. But when young women are thrown to the wolves in the business world, they often dither too much. They want each report to be perfect and fuss over it too long. They don't answer questions unless they know the answer with certainty. Bob Sullivan and Hugh Thompson, the authors of *The Plateau Effect*, call this tendency the "enemy of the good," leading as it does to hours of wasted time. The irony is that striving to be perfect actually keeps us from getting much of anything done.

Get it as good as you can and then move on.

There is a lot of data out there that women often do not apply for jobs or promotions unless they meet every criterion. If they are not a perfect match, they do not apply. Men are not as hung up on perfection and rarely limit themselves. Men take risks. Cowgirls, like our Dell clients, understand that there are times when you get it about 80 percent right and go for it. This does not mean you settle for the imperfect solution. It means you prioritize action over perfection. Take action and work on making it better over time. General George Patton once said, "A good plan, violently executed now, is better than a perfect plan executed next week."

COWGIRLS MAKE THEIR OWN RULES

Many of the cowgirls highlighted in this book just plain marched to the beat of a different drummer. They left boarding school to join a rodeo or a Wild West show. They chose to work with the cowboys on their family ranches instead of staying in the house and helping their mothers cook. They were not afraid to break the rules every now and then. I admire this spunk and have to admit I have broken a few rules and conventions in my career and life. Some of those times put me in the absolute best place to win and of course have given me great personal satisfaction.

One female university student told me she decided to major in marketing. Her family, close friends, and advisors all had insisted she major in accounting and pursue a career in finance. Although it took a lot of courage on her part to deny their wishes and dreams for her, she was thrilled with her decision to do something she really thought she would enjoy. This takes grit. She is already becoming a cowgirl. Bravo!

What I am suggesting is that just because everyone is zigging, perhaps you should zag. Don't be afraid to think about ways no one else has done things before. Make your own rules. It is your life and nobody else can do this for you.

GO WITH PEOPLE WHO PULL YOU FORWARD

I learned this lesson early in my career when I accepted the job with Leadership Dynamics that taught me so much about the importance of personality types. I had several other job offers at the time, but I thought I would learn more working with them in their executive consulting practice.

They hired me because of my marketing background; they wanted me to help them grow their business, and I did. But very quickly I got involved in their consulting projects. At first I was just writing case studies for marketing purposes. The insights fascinated me and taught me an entirely new way of thinking and interacting with people. Soon, I was writing proposals, giving presentations, and interacting directly with many of the executives.

The Harvard MBAs inspired me, showed me the way, and changed my life. Those are the kind of people you want to hang out with. Time is your most precious asset; spend it with people who inspire you. Run away from anyone else. This is an important lesson to learn early in life. In this day of social media, focus on the quality of people you spend time with, not the quantity, which can steal your mental energy. Have lunch with people you admire. Get to know them better. Ask questions. Reach out and, for goodness' sake, follow up.

Do not follow the crowd, especially if you feel something is wrong. Once, in grade school during rehearsal for a ballet recital, I fell in with some girls who trashed a school bathroom with theatrical paint. My parents were horrified, disappointed, and devastated that I used such poor judgment. I never did anything like that again, but I still wake up from bad dreams remembering how upset they were with me.

If you want to become a powerful person, hang out with people with powerful ambitions. Find interesting people from all walks of life who are doing inspirational things, and include them in a network that helps all of you. Friendship is always a two-way street. Maintaining a relationship with someone you admire, even if it is distant, is a smart, healthy thing to do. And it is the highest compliment that you can pay someone to check in on them from time to time to see how they are doing.

With today's technology it is much easier to do, just be sure that you take the time to put some heart into your communications. Share your creativity, your learning, and your insights with the people you know and care about. But don't forget the power of handwritten notes. George H. W. Bush told a friend of mine, "I got to the White House with one handwritten note at a time."

And help people when you can. I have built an amazing network of powerful women I know all over the world through C200. We have a rule that we never solicit business from each other. But when one of them reaches out saying her daughter is looking for a new job, I'm all over it. I recently got one young woman six stellar interviews at the kind of organizations she wanted to work for. She got the job she wanted. One more drop in the bucket of goodwill! I try to be very honest about my ability to help. I cannot do it all, but for a close friend, if I can, I pull out all the stops.

THE DISARMING POWER OF SOUTHERN CHARM

I was raised with a sense of Southern charm and power. We were taught that when visiting to always arrive with a gift, write thank-you notes to the hosts, and when hosting have place cards at the dinner table. We said "Yes, sir" and "No, ma'am." That's just how we were raised.

When T3 purchased the Pope-Watson mansion in Austin, we poured on the Southern charm and made it a part of our brand. When clients came to town, there was always a small gift waiting for them in their hotel room. There were handmade place cards at the dinner table, and the evenings always ended with a round of toasts. I used my calligraphy skills to write thank-you notes to our clients and staff. In fact, I gave a handwritten birthday and anniversary card to each T3 employee until I turned over the reins of writing these notes to Ben, our oldest son and the president of T3 today. People need to know that you appreciate them on a personal level. When clients come to the ranch we roll out a turn-of-the-century chuck wagon and serve up family-style Texas barbeque.

Making people feel welcome and appreciated is somewhat of a lost art. Be a warm, generous host. Go a little further to be a genuine and an authentic cowgirl. One of my senior team members at T3 tells the story about how she once saw me standing barefoot in our ranch kitchen at midnight peeling hard-boiled eggs with our clients from Microsoft. They were spending a few days with us and wanted to make deviled eggs from the Double Heart Ranch's free-range chickens. That's about as authentic as it gets.

Sometimes Southern charm can be a bit much. One of Ben and Sam Gaddis's cousins interned with us at T3 for a few years. He grew up pretty country and I would cringe when I would hear him answering the telephone and responding with "okeydokey." But he was authentic and I never stopped him!

STOP AND KISS THE CLOWN

If you have ever been to a rodeo, you have seen the rodeo clown. They have been delighting audiences for years and more importantly, their real mission is to protect bull riders from being stomped on by bucking bulls after they finish a ride. They have saved many lives and are the real heroes of the rodeos. They make it look easy, but it is not. Rodeo clowning is no laughing matter.

I saw a talented girl at a rodeo run the best time of the night in barrel racing. She turned in a stellar performance. It was clear she was going to be the winner and pretty much the star of the evening. When she heard her time called over the loudspeaker she whooped a big whoop, jumped off her horse, and ran over and kissed the rodeo clown on the lips. The audience roared with approval as she climbed back on her horse and took a victory lap. I was in awe of her. Not only had she won through years of hard work and practice, but she had the moxie to leverage her win by recognizing the clown and sharing the limelight with him. By doing so she gained respect and power, and everyone in attendance that night knew it.

Kiss the clown. Take the time to stop and recognize your team. Give them all of the credit. Thank them. You'll be a powerful cowgirl when you do.

Lessons Learned: Cowgirls Are Responsible for Themselves

- The ability to stand back and see yourself clearly and objectively is incredibly powerful. Cowgirls are not afraid of constructive criticism, and welcome it if it makes them better. If you confront your own reality, both good and bad, you gain authentic insight.
- Dreams are the opposite of reality; they can take you anywhere. The magic comes when the real YOU intersects with YOUR dreams. Pathways to the future quickly emerge.

Annie Oakley
(The National Annie Oakley Center at Garst Museum, Greenville, Ohio)

Chapter 5

COWGIRLS BUILD THEIR OWN COMPETENCE

When it comes to competence, one woman stands out. Annie Oakley. To paraphrase legendary football coach Bum Phillips, if she isn't in a class by herself, when that class gets together, it sure don't take long to call the roll.

She was America's first female superstar, and she was a true rags to riches story. She was born in 1860 and her father died when she was six. Her family was so poor she taught herself to shoot and began hunting animals for food. She even got so good that she could shoot an animal without ruining the best parts of the meat. She started selling the meat her family didn't need and by age fifteen had made enough money to pay off the bank loan for her family's farm.

On Thanksgiving Day, 1875, Frank Butler was out promoting his traveling shooting exhibition scheduled that evening in Cincinnati. As he often did, he struck up a wager with a prominent local businessman. The two men bet one hundred dollars that Frank could outshoot anyone in the city. There was much boasting and bravado, and a crowd started to build in anticipation of who would take on this famous marksman. Out stepped a five-foot-tall, fifteen-year-old girl named Phoebe Ann Mosey. Frank laughed when he saw her. He did not laugh for long, because to his surprise, she scored twenty-five hits in twenty-five attempts. Frank did as well, but his last shot kicked the target outside of the designated area. So she won. The crowd loved it. Frank was a good sport and invited Phoebe to his show that night. He married her a year later.[8]

On May 1, 1882, in Springfield, Illinois, Frank's stage partner was ill and could not perform so he asked Phoebe to hold up his targets. He was having a bad night and kept missing his shots. Someone in the crowd shouted, "Let the girl shoot, let her shoot!" Phoebe did not hesitate. She stepped right on the stage and hit all of her targets. The crowd loved it and a star was born that night. She quickly moved to top billing and Frank became her manager. Around this time, Phoebe adopted her new stage name as "Annie Oakley."[9]

Between 1885 and 1901 Annie Oakley starred in Buffalo Bill's Wild West show as an exhibition shooter. She quickly became the first female Wild West star. The most amazing thing about Annie is how good she really was. While she spent most of her life on the stage doing exhibitions, she also shot in serious marksman competitions. She chalked up remarkable records, shooting 483 out of 500, 943 out of 1,000. In one single day she shot 4,772 out of 5,000.[10] Annie knew how to please the crowd by blowing kisses and making fun of herself by dramatically pouting and stomping her foot when she missed a shot.

Oh, and I was in a musical about her when I was in high school—*Annie Get Your Gun*. I can still sing all the words of the songs today!

Cowgirls understand that they have many lessons to learn. They have a curiosity and passion to not only learn, but also to become the best they can be, constantly improving. Practice, observing the teachings from those who have gone before you, and sheer determination will lead to competence. Instead of reinventing the wheel, cowgirls learn early in life there is a right and wrong way to do things. From the family dogma of standing by your word and always doing what you say you will do, to the seemingly smaller yet sometimes life-saving technique of tying a proper quick-release knot. (In case you don't know what a quick-release knot is, it is the correct way to tie up a horse so if it spooks, you can release it quickly so the animal doesn't injure itself.) Cowgirls know that these lessons are based on generations of pride, character, safety, and strong family values.

COWGIRLS DO THE WORK TO LEARN

Cowgirls know that horses have a sixth sense that people do not. Horses are prey animals and they are always judging how safe they are. I have been around horses all my life and I have seen it over and over again. One person can approach a horse and it will appear to be skittish. It will turn its head, pin its ears back, and try to move away. Another person can approach that same horse and it will step forward and put its head down to have its ears scratched. Why the difference? Horses can sense both fear and expertise almost instantly. Horses sense body language, adrenaline levels, and just about everything going on around them.

Because of their intuition, a horse senses how much a rider knows before she climbs into the saddle. And how much she does not know. The horse always judges the rider. After the young cowgirl learns the basic skills, she must win the horse's trust and make the animal feel safe around her. The horse has to trust that she will not put it in danger. It takes time; it takes kindness.

Once she wins its trust, girls and horses relate to each other in magical, mystical ways that men do not see and do not understand. Horses can be headstrong, stubborn, ill-tempered, and dangerous (like a lot of men), but they are usually complete pushovers when they encounter a young girl with a halter on her shoulder and a big grin on her face. We saw this every day with our daughter, Rebecca. Cowgirls earn a horse's trust. By perfecting each technique, she becomes more competent. As she learns, she is more assured of her knowledge and skills, and that gradually builds confidence. It continues in a virtuous circle, building trust and competence at the same time. And as the months go by, that confidence emerges as assertiveness. I have watched a bond of trust develop between these young women and their animals. Hard work, learning the right way to do every little detail, and sitting high in the saddle steadily build inner strength and also physical stamina. I am always amazed at how these girls develop their own personal power.

As that power develops and skills are honed, many of these girls decide to compete. They compete in dressage, western riding, jumping, barrel racing, and more. They ride hard and they understand winning and losing. A select few end up decked out in glittery hats and tight pants, riding into a rodeo arena on their horse carrying the American flag while someone makes another brave attempt at "The Star-Spangled Banner." All my life, I dreamed it would be me, but my mom wasn't too keen on seeing all those pesky cowboys seeking my attention.

THE CONFIDENCE GAP

I have read much of the literature and attended many conferences about women's issues in business. One of the first things
you always hear about is the confidence gap—that women
don't feel sure about their leadership abilities, that they are
hesitant to take risks, that they are not outspoken and tend to
stay back, don't push, don't challenge. They do not push for
promotions or raises as effectively as men do. That does not
sound like the cowgirl way!

Immediately, women are treated differently. Everyone is on
high alert. Nostrils flare. When does a well-meant criticism
cross the line and become harassment? I know that many men
in business are less likely to correct women than they are men.
Too often, men miss an opportunity to offer well-intended
criticism, which means that women miss the opportunity to
learn. If that happens over and over, it may not be such a surprise why women tend to lose confidence after their first year
or two at work. They often get left off of the invitation list to
activities their male counterparts participate in. If a woman is
included, the men have to watch what they say. Fun over.

I have frequently put my male counterparts at ease by
talking about the highlights of a football game, or using
candor or homespun humor to make a point. If I describe
something that is stronger than bear's breath, then they
know they don't have to walk on eggshells around me.
Don't try this unless you can really be authentic, but if you
can, it is pretty powerful.

So what's the difference between these women and my
cowgirls? No one worried about shouting at cowgirls when
they made a mistake, because they would just grin and holler
back. Many women today have not grown up in the rough-

and-tumble world of cowgirls, are not used to well-meaning criticism, and as a result, they don't handle it well. So women have a tendency to stay in safe places. That choice makes them seem unengaged and indecisive.

To compound the problem is the fact that some women's use of language makes them seem tentative and uncertain. Phrases like "I think" or "I just" slip into the discourse.[11] I recently did several focus groups at different universities, and many of the young women I spoke with used "I think" every few minutes. Stop it! Women tend to talk too fast and without enough emphasis on key points. And then there is that deadliest of all communications sins, up talking. You have all heard this. It is when a person's voice pitch lilts up at the end of a sentence. It makes the statement seem indecisive and weak. I say no to this! Hire a speech therapist if you suffer from this debilitating affliction.

So women are often afraid to speak up, to take risks. Men are afraid to give them a hand and help them improve because it might come across as sexist and demeaning. What a mess! There is no single villain here. Most of the men I know are actually drawn to strong, powerful women, and champion them. And I don't believe there are a lot of women out there who would not like to lead successful lives.

I have read articles about building confidence that suggest you can just decide to be confident, like it is a learned behavior. "Stand up straight, lower your voice, slow down," I have heard them all. Sorry, it does not work that way. Authentic confidence means being true to yourself about what you have actually achieved, not how you are perceived. You have to believe that you have important ideas and perspectives. You have to believe that you have earned the right to express them. Your competence comes from your talent, education, and contributions to your team. Then confidence follows right along.

There is no way around this. If you want to be more powerful, you are going to have to know more than anyone else in the room. You have to do your research and think things through. You cannot fake it. You do not have to do it all yourself; build up your team to help you. But you must have vision, insight, and conviction in what you bring to the table. If you don't, you will not be authentic. It simply does not work.

If you are not confident in your own competence, then focus all of your energy on yourself for a while. Learn new things. Become an expert. It takes time, hard work, and dedication. Then you will earn real respect and admiration. Your confidence will come, and when it does, you will become a powerful, assertive character who is authentic because she has done the work. There are many ways to build your confidence, but few shortcuts. *Competence breeds confidence, which breeds assertiveness, which breeds more personal power, which breeds more flexibility for a successful life.*

HELP OTHERS WHILE GROWING YOUR CONFIDENCE

My company has always done a lot of pro bono work through the years—everything from supporting the local opera to helping with abused children to feeding the homeless. Early in T3's history the Salvation Army had built a new facility in downtown Austin but because of the downturn in the economy, many people were not able to meet the financial pledges they had made during better times. A few people on the board of directors asked me if T3 would do an advertising campaign to help fill the contribution gap.

This came at a time when I was just starting the business and, quite honestly, we didn't have the time or resources to do it, but we did anyway.

For the print portion of our Salvation Army campaign, we came up with a brilliant idea. It would require a centerfold spread in the *Austin American-Statesman*, which was not cheap. I made an appointment with the editor in chief at the *Statesman*, walked into his office, and shared the concept about helping homeless people with him. The copy simply said: "To You It's a Newspaper. To the Homeless It's a Blanket."

Wow.

The editor bought into the concept. In fact, he loved it. I asked him to donate the centerfold in the Sunday paper two weeks from then. He gulped, and sat there for a minute. Finally, he said, "OK. I will give you the tabloid section." I looked back at him and said, "That is the size of a paper towel." It was more like a rag than a blanket. I needed the centerfold to be in the main section of the newspaper, to almost be the size of a blanket. Again, we sat there. I practiced one of the most important rules of negotiations—he who speaks first, loses. I just shut up and looked at him. Finally, he said, "OK. You got it."

When I walked out the door, I felt powerful. I had used just a few words and silence to accomplish my goal. It turned out to be one of the most impactful ads we ever did. We won a national ADDY for the campaign and also raised an amazing amount of money and saved the Salvation Army's Austin building. And, of course, I ended up serving on the Salvation Army board of directors for many years.

I walked a little taller after this experience. For young people just starting out in life, nonprofit organizations represent wonderful opportunities to learn, grow, and help you better understand what you are good at. And what makes you happy.

Helping with nonprofits is a way to build power that is accessible to everyone, regardless of your position in life, and it is a great way to expand your network. I volunteered extensively starting in high school well into my early career and met some wonderful characters and lifelong friends, like Dick Rathgeber, who I served with on the Salvation Army board. Dick once told me, "If ten percent of the people aren't pissed off at you at any given time, then you ain't really doin' bizness!"

Learning how nonprofits work is an invaluable experience in motivating people, understanding governance, and doing good. You work with people who are volunteering, so you already have something in common—a unifying objective. Learn to lead people. These are relatively safe environments; your teammates are not going to let you fail. Spread your wings and see what you can make happen. Prove yourself here and you will be better prepared for what is next in your life. And you will have topped off those buckets of goodwill.

Another breakthrough think tank idea was born at the cross section of need and a new technology. In 2009, mobile texting was new and was foreign to the ad community as a way of funding or selling anything. We wanted to help our friend Alan Graham with his Mobile Loaves & Fishes nonprofit. He had been feeding the homeless on the streets of Austin but was ready to take his mission one step further by helping the homeless get housing and build a long-term community.

We had this wild idea of raising a homeless man hundreds of feet in the air, and standing him on an outdoor billboard that was on I-35, one of the busiest highways in the country. So for two days, Danny stood in front of that billboard that simply read, "I am Danny. I am homeless. I am HERE," with an arrow pointing to Danny. It also said, "1,200 texts gets me a home," and "Text 'Danny' to 20222 to donate $10."

Danny got a home. He was reunited with his daughter, who had lost track of him and saw him on the national news. And the results for Mobile Loaves & Fishes were nothing short of staggering:

- 33 percent increase in total year-over-year donations
- 300 percent increase in online donors
- 575 percent increase in MLF.org site traffic
- $12,000 in local mobile donations in forty-eight hours
- $606,000 more MLF donations than the previous year

The campaign generated 333 news stories in thirty-two markets reaching nearly 13 million viewers thanks to CNN, Fox News, the *Huffington Post*, *USA Today*, MSN, and more.

And the best result of all? One reunited family.

UNDERSTANDING WHERE PEOPLE ARE COMING FROM

I have written about my dad's philosophy of meeting people where they are. Here is an example of how I used it:

Not long after I arrived at the advertising agency Fellers, Lacy & Gaddis, I had a very outspoken client who was producing an annual report. We assigned a copywriter to work with him on the project. The first time they met, he talked nearly nonstop for almost an hour. My copywriter took notes and said very little. After the meeting the client stopped me in the hall and said, "That woman is dull and maybe stupid. She did not react at all. I want another copywriter." Later that afternoon, I ran into the copywriter, who said, "What a pompous bore he is."

I knew I was in trouble. So at the next meeting I did a quick team-building exercise with MBTI personality assessment. The bottom line was that the client was a huge extrovert and the copywriter was a huge introvert. I suggested we let him talk and let her listen and process, and then give her a couple of days to collect her thoughts and give him a written response.

We all agreed. A few days later she walked into the meeting with the first draft of the entire annual report. He sat in silence and read it. He looked up at both of us and said, "Brilliant!" The two of them became fast friends and big collaborators. From that point forward, he would arrive at a meeting, pontificate, and then leave with no expectations of an immediate reaction from her. He was confident that when she absorbed his thoughts and had time to organize them, her response would be spot-on. They both learned that they actually worked better together because they were total opposites, and I hung on to the business.

People are different; we all know that. But why? Brothers and sisters who grow up in the same exact environment turn out to be totally different people. Some of us, like me, are big extroverts. Others prefer to think before they speak. We don't know why this is true, but it is. One of the best ways to understand this fact is to take the MBTI assessment. I would suggest girls take it midway through high school and learn the principles. Then do it again midway through college and again when you are starting your career. I know from experience that young people's type can shift in subtle ways, so doing it several times really helps. I promise it will be one of the most important things you can do to better understand yourself and how you instinctively deal with other people. And it's a lot of fun. Go to www.myersbriggs.org for more information.

The MBTI will show you your preferred use of perception and judgment and will make you understand people who deal with information in different ways than you do. I have seen it open people's eyes over and over. It gives you a mental framework to understand where people are coming from. Always remember, it is more of a ZIP code to your personality, not a street address.

If I am talking to an SJ (sensing-judging type, which makes up more than half of the population), I know I can't be vague or esoteric. I have to show a clear path, timeline, and result. If I'm talking to an NT (intuitive-thinking type), I can be more metaphorical—present in a more complex, inventive way. I can talk about what the future could be.

This one skill makes you radically more powerful because you develop shortcuts for effectively communicating with different personality types.

WHAT DO YOU DO BETTER THAN ANYONE ELSE?

Find your passion in life, embrace it, and become an expert at it. For cowgirls, this usually involves a horse! Becoming an expert at something you love may be a lifelong calling, or it may be an interest that you pursue for just a few months. In either case it means being curious, actively learning something that can make you smarter or simply more interesting. We have so much to learn and so little time.

Digging deep into something builds character and signals intelligence, grit, and self-reliance. At the University of Texas, I developed a passion for black-and-white photography after taking a class that Garry Winogrand taught. Winogrand was a street photographer in New York and had a dramatic, almost intrusive style that I loved. I learned to shoot close up, almost invading people's space. I learned how to use light and exposure and how to dodge prints in the darkroom. I would find myself in the darkroom most of the night—getting back to my dorm at 3 a.m. Time flies when you are doing something you are passionate about.

Being inspired by Winogrand's work and winning his praise for my photographs (which was no small task since he didn't hand out compliments easily), I truly knew that, for the first time in college, I had excelled at something that I loved to do. My work was even shown around the University of Texas campus as examples of fine art.

The summer after one of his classes, I traveled to Europe and took wonderful black-and-white photographs that are still displayed in our home today. And visitors never fail to admire them. I look at those images that I took in Europe some forty years ago and am amazed at how much character and raw emotion I was able to capture at such a young age. That summer I was able to meet wonderful people on the streets of small towns all over Italy and become a powerful photographer.

A few years ago, the Metropolitan Museum of Art in New York created an exhibit of hundreds of Winogrand's photographs, most that had never been seen by the public. As I took all of this in, tears welled up in my eyes. I realized that through my photography (which I have kept up with all of my life), I have learned to perfect something. It has revealed a lot about my tenacity, and being able to stick with something. It has made me a more fascinating person and has helped me make connections with interesting people and embrace new ideas in our ever-changing world.

RUB ON SOME SELF-DEPRECATING HUMOR

Powerful people lift people's spirits. They make it fun for people to work together. As a manager I could always sense the collective mood of T3. But as I matured as a manager I learned not only to sense it, but also to build on it. You crack a joke, tell a funny story, say thank you, ask about the old family dog. You engage and find a way to move the mood.

Years ago we had a telephone system with a paging feature, which we rarely used. But on Friday afternoons, when things started to wind down, I would hit the "Page" button and play recordings of famous movie lines, like "Sell crazy someplace else, we're all stocked up here." People howled with laughter. And soon others would chime in with ridiculous songs and sounds. They would all head home for the weekend with smiles on their faces, which I loved.

Not long after e-mail came on the scene, one of our technical guys sent one that said, "I lost my dongle. It is small and purple. Let me know if you find it." A hush went through the building as people read that cryptic message, quickly followed by a big collective laugh. A sense of humor, especially self-deprecating, is just plain attractive. Life is tough enough, so why not inject a little humor and a smile in almost everything you do?

Our Double Heart Ranch foreman, Hardy Vaughn, is a master at this. Many times, if one of our Texas Longhorn cows is slightly overweight, he will say something like, "She is getting a belly on her about as big as mine."

Today, we have replaced our telephone paging system with Slack, a messaging platform. Now we have video snippets from social media, TV shows, and movies flowing across our computers, making it hard not to laugh. We even have one team member who has set up her own advice channel, where she will answer people's questions on virtually any subject. She's a cowgirl.

ALWAYS HAVE A POINT OF VIEW

Having a strong point of view demonstrates your competence, that you have thought things through. I know a lot of women who are not comfortable around conflict. They just don't like it. But properly managed conflict is invaluable and something most women need to be more comfortable with because it forces you to articulate your personal values and beliefs.

I watch my three Border Collies at the ranch. Several times a day they tie into one another. It is a very aggressive form of play and usually stops short of drawing blood. They grab each other around the neck, knock each other down, growl and snarl at each other. It is the most natural thing in the world, because they are practicing their aggressive skills for a time when they need to make a kill or defend themselves. It keeps their skills honed. And strangely enough, it is most likely to happen when we are on a conference call at the ranch because they are spoiled and want our full attention.

People need the same exercise, maybe with less teeth. I admire people with strong points of view. I do not have to agree with them, but I respect someone who has done the mental gymnastics to form a strong opinion, and that usually means debating the pros and cons of issues. Too often, women shy away from debates and it is a mistake. Force yourself to verbally argue out an issue. It is the only way to form strong opinions. If you cannot take a challenge, you probably have not thought through an issue or done your homework. I learned a lot about points of view because back in my high school debate classes I had to argue from one point of view and then turn right around and argue from the opposite perspective. Debate, and then you will be ready to have a strong point of view that people will want to hear.

The Roman Catholic Church understood this when they appointed a "devil's advocate" to present arguments against a proposed beatification or canonization. They were worried that they had too many yes-men making important decisions. Find someone to argue with. Be challenged. Be OK being uncomfortable. It is an amazing confidence builder.

Ask yourself, when was the last time you had a healthy, robust debate? Find your partner, get two glasses of wine, jump in the hot tub, and debate like a cowgirl.

WHEN YOU SPEAK, LEAD WITH YOUR HEART

I have always been comfortable on my feet in front of a crowd. Some of it comes from my mother thrusting me into almost every event and parade in East Texas. My husband says that I never miss an opportunity to run in front of a parade. In fact, I just entered the dog parade in nearby Burnet, Texas, dressed up in a beaded black evening gown, beautiful black heels, and long white gloves, walking my beloved, ever so handsome black-and-white Aussie and Border Collie mix named Henry, who was sporting a black bow tie. He looked like he had on a tuxedo. I thought we were adorable and would surely come home with the blue ribbon, but a country and western hound dog act beat us out! If you put yourself out there, sometimes you are going to get beat!

I have given speeches all over the world—to a closed audience of sixteen amazingly wealthy women in Dubai to over a thousand in Tampa, to business students in China and on many college campuses. I usually have a few slides to keep me on the topic of the presentation and to illustrate the points I am trying to make, but I always speak extemporaneously. I usually know a lot about what I am talking about, so it is pretty easy for me. And I keep the audience energized and laughing with a few of my crazy stories. But often I will step away from the lectern or walk out into the crowd and genuinely speak from my heart. Those moments are never planned. They come from watching what resonates with the audience in real time. These moments are always about emotional connections. I know when I get to one. I stop and I talk candidly about it.

I am amazed at the feedback I get from those moments. People say they have rarely heard someone speak with more authenticity, or who was more genuine or open about her feelings. I get notes and e-mails saying kind and wonderful things, and it always touches me deeply. I know speaking is intimidating for a lot of people, but work at it and do not be afraid to put your heart into it and show your passion and even vulnerability. If you speak the truth, you don't have to be perfect. People won't care.

When I was working for Leadership Dynamics in Atlanta, I took an evening speech class at Emory University. I have a pretty strong East Texas accent. I asked my professor if I needed to lose the accent to be effective. He said, "Everyone has an accent. It's not as important how you sound as it is what you have to say." So my Texas twang is still here.

Work on your presentation style. Join Toastmasters and other speech groups. Be yourself, speak with your own authentic voice. But slow down. Walk around, take control of the room. Use some humor. Be introspective. Be warm. Make your audience relax. Be heard. Let them see the cowgirl that you are.

If there is one piece of advice I could give to those of you with children, it would be to introduce them to situations where they can learn to be comfortable speaking in public. It will serve them well in life, build their confidence, and make them powerful people.

IT'S OK TO BE INTIMIDATED NOW AND THEN

When I spent the week with the military, one morning before daylight we boarded buses and went to Parris Island, South Carolina, where marine recruits have their first exposure to US Marine Corps drill instructors. As we climbed out of the bus, the drill instructors started yelling at us, treating us as if we were raw recruits. We followed the yellow footprints on the pavement where thousands of marine recruits have stood through the years. We tried to follow orders as best we could. But, I have to admit to you, I was totally intimidated. I was so shaken that when they handed out rations I spilled my box of cereal on the floor. My drill instructor was not very gracious about it!

I recently had dinner at the French embassy in Washington, DC, with a group of powerful people who were working on finding better ways to work together on both sides of the political aisle by focusing on areas where we can agree. It was a lovely dinner and I felt pretty much at ease. I was raised a Southern girl and knew my table manners, but there were multiple knives and forks that I had rarely seen before. I looked at the other people and quickly saw they were experiencing the same dilemma. We all laughed at once, and I asked one of the waiters to explain the protocol to us savages. He was very accommodating.

Being intimidated is not a bad thing. It keeps you on your toes and honest about what you do and don't know. People that intimidate me are usually ones who have a particular expertise that I don't have. They can be from backgrounds, organizations, and situations with which I am not familiar. However, once I get to know these people, we usually hit it off and learn from each other.

I have come to believe that if you are not occasionally intimidated, you are not trying hard enough. You are not putting yourself out there as much as you should. Find someone you are in awe of and find a way to go see them. Sure it can be a little scary, but do it anyway.

Oh, did I mention that I am intimidated by rattlesnakes? Thank goodness I am a great shot.

NEVER STOP LEARNING OR TEACHING

One of our creative leaders has been with us for many years, and from time to time we worried that he might have a hard time keeping up with all of the changes we have experienced in the business. Just about the time you think he might be lagging a bit, he reinvents himself and emerges with something completely new. He has done it more times than Madonna. He listens, and he reads constantly. He is a quick study. He is self-aware, not the best manager in the world, and a big introvert. But when clients meet him, they beg for him to work on their projects. Literally.

T3 has always been a learning environment, and we are led by many self-taught people. Don't wait on someone else to teach you; go learn it yourself. Make the effort, put the time into it, and get better. One of the most important skills a woman needs to develop as she progresses through her career, especially after her children are more self-sufficient, is honing her learning ability. To keep your mind fresh, have a lifelong learning strategy and learn at least two new competencies every year.

Inventory your skills and decide where to focus your learning. From a career perspective, there is always something to learn and usually pretty awesome videos and courses to help you do it. From a personal perspective, follow your passions and increase your expertise every year. *A cowgirl is always working on a new trick with her horse.* Practice, practice, practice.

Lessons Learned: Cowgirls Build Their Own Competence

- There are no shortcuts to becoming competent. You have to be relentless, fearless, and dedicated when it comes to tackling the work and steps it will take to gain your competencies. Associate yourself with people smarter and better than you, and you will reach new heights. I was in the audience when Nancy Lopez (the renowned professional golfer) said in her speech, "You have to play with people better than you or you will never up your own game." This is true in business and life. She won forty-eight LPGA tour events! And, by the way, I think Nancy is a cowgirl.

- As Nancy's example points out, to excel, you have to do things better than anyone else. Find those talents and spend your life building upon them. Mix in a little optimism and serendipity, and you have the formula for success.

Mildred Douglas Chrisman
(National Cowgirl Museum and Hall of Fame, Fort Worth, Texas)

Chapter 6

COWGIRLS USE COMPETENCE TO FIND CONFIDENCE

Let me introduce you to one true crowd-pleaser. Mildred Douglas Chrisman just wasn't cut out to stay in a stodgy Connecticut boarding school. However, they did teach horseback riding as part of the curriculum, and she decided she liked horses better than books. So she left school and joined the circus! Barnum and Bailey's, to be exact, which led to an opportunity at the 101 Ranch Wild West show.

Mildred teaches us that sometimes you just must take a leap of faith. Go with your gut and courageously follow your dreams. One step of change will lead you to the next opportunity.

Not only did Mildred take that leap, but she was a real winner. In 1918, she won championships in Cheyenne and Pendleton. Bronc and steer riding were her sports, along with trick riding and trick shooting. Her dangerous relay races and bucking horse competitions worked the crowds into a frenzy of yelling, cheers, and applause. Not a demure bone in her body! Her personal brand was enhanced with flashy, fringed skirts and vests. Mildred was a master of winning over crowds from one road show to the next.

Cowgirls like Mildred learned to be extremely confident in their rodeo performances. But to become a superstar, you have to be willing to differentiate yourself and win over your audience time and time again. Once you have that down, it is much easier to assert yourself in situations where before you might have shied away. Building on competence doesn't always make you qualified to be assertive, but pick your battles in this arena and you will eventually win the war.

YOU DON'T JUST THINK YOU CAN. YOU KNOW YOU CAN.

Cowgirls have learned to be tough, but they are still very much women and act like women. Cowgirls have the power to assume both masculine and feminine traits when it suits them. They have the ability to go back and forth—to be vulnerable at some times and bold at other times. On top of this, they have the self-confidence to laugh at themselves for doing it. What emerges is irresistible. Men can't do this, so this is a wonderful, unfair advantage.

Research published in *Insights* by Stanford Graduate School of Business, "Researchers: How Women Can Succeed in the Workplace" shows that women who are aggressive, assertive, and confident, but who can turn these traits on and off, depending on social situations, get more promotions than either men or other women. In many ways, women who learn to do this become more powerful than most men, according to the research.[12]

A woman who can take a powerful stand, laugh about it, and then slide back into her gracious feminine charm has a raw power that can disarm almost anyone. I have had this ability most of my life. I can play both roles pretty well. At this point, I do it instinctively. If this behavior isn't instinctive for you, here is what I recommend. Try this out first with family or your Rough Rider colleagues. Learn to push the pedal and take a strong stand, then slip back in to a more kind, sensitive person. As my mother said, "Kill them with kindness."

Being a bit of a chameleon by playing both feminine and masculine roles can help you find a business voice that works for you.

BE ASSERTIVE—SOLVE A PROBLEM

Solving problems gives you the authority to be assertive. The more you do it, the more power you earn, and the more trust you build. At T3, our clients bring us their marketing problems every day. In the early days of my career it was often difficult, if not impossible, to prove that an advertising campaign actually worked. My team had opinions, our clients had opinions, but there was not a lot of supporting data on either side. Generally, if a client liked his TV commercial and it connected (either made them laugh or cry) with his board of directors, and his buddies on the golf course said, "Hey, I really like your TV spot!" it was deemed a success.

As we moved into the digital space we began to develop better ways of proving up results. We could measure sales. We could measure page views, the time spent on a particular page and as a result we got much better at proving success. We moved from opinions about results to actual data about results. Now we have so much information that the challenge becomes determining which data points are the most important. Our analytics team can run reports on massive data sets searching for correlations we never dreamed existed. That is a powerful tool we deliver to our clients.

So today we test concepts, media mix, price offers—all kinds of things—and we have developed the skills to forecast how campaigns will perform. There is nothing more exciting than to launch a campaign and watch the results come in, in real time. We see the data pour in and we learn what mobile app ad pulls the best, what media delivers the most effective return on investment. It is like election night every day at T3.

Most of the decisions we make are fairly logical, but we have learned not to stop at logic. We push through with things we do not completely understand. Do customers react better to different typefaces? Are two offers more engaging than one? Does an illustration work better than a photograph for this specific information? Where is the best place for the "Buy" button on the page?

These learnings provide our clients with real solutions. Provable solutions. Our constant learning gives our clients power in their organizations. They do not have to say, "I think." They can stand up and say, "I know." This is simply raw power. It gives them the authority to bulldoze a lot of office politics and push their agenda forward.

Every day look for ways to prove the value of what you do. Measure it. Work to make it better. You will learn more and your confidence will soar. Your results will improve your competence. Do it over and over again. Your ongoing optimization proves you are gaining more competence. What a wonderful little virtuous circle for a cowgirl to ride into.

DON'T STAND THERE WITH HAT IN HAND

In South Texas there is an old saying, "Don't stand there with hat in hand." In the ranching world, cowboys did not take off their hat unless talking to a lady, or someone who could be considered superior to them. Or unless they were putting pride aside and asking for something, usually money.

Warm Springs Rehabilitation Hospital was a client of ours for many years. It was a small account, but we believed in their mission. It originated in the 1930s as a polio treatment facility. After polio was largely eliminated, their mission shifted to helping people with traumatic brain injuries. They were wonderful, caring people who stood up and took care of some of the most challenging cases— bringing people as far back as possible from devastating brain injuries. Many of them were the victims of motorcycle accidents.

They had one very nice, semiretired man who was their fund-raiser. He stopped by our office one day for coffee and confided in me that he was having a real challenge getting through to potential donors. He said, "I feel like I go in asking for money with my hat in hand." The feeling he was expressing to me was that he did not feel any sense of power. It broke my heart.

I was determined to fix it because I knew the power of what the hospital did. I had worked for them for years and was a true believer. We built a complete fund-raising system for him that told the story of the original mission, of the win against polio and the bravery of both the caretakers and the patients. The messages were beautiful, sobering, inspirational, and they worked. The tools we gave him enabled him to find his own personal power by being able to tell an effective, emotional story about the need. He was never standing "hat in hand" again; instead he had a strong, emotional, authentic story that was worthy of serious consideration.

Cowgirls understand that they have to be assertive if they want to manage their own lives. They understand that life is a series of negotiations on almost every level. The terms "negotiation" and "power" conjure up a lot of negative, business-oriented imagery—fat, cigar-smoking men in stinky rooms making deals to only benefit themselves. I understand that. That is precisely why a lot of women shy away from thinking about how to be more powerful when they have these important conversations.

When you go into a negotiation, I want you to go in with your hat firmly planted on your head. I want you to go in confidently with as much power as possible, not to try to beat the other person, but to be able to stand up for yourself and find a win-win solution. Go in with pride about your accomplishments and skills. Go in as a strong team leader who has lifted people up. Go in as someone people trust. Go in with facts and figures and make a compelling argument. Go in prepared. And with all of your personal power behind you.

Go make a good deal, cowgirl.

UNDERSTAND HOW THE MONEY WORKS

You absolutely must understand the financial basics of your organization. Not understanding them will make you crazy. It's like trying to play a game without knowing the rules. I made a point early in my career to reach out to Bill Lacy and ask him to teach me the basics of the advertising business. I mastered them and built the biggest book of business in the firm.

For years after I started my own business and we computerized our financial system, I kept my own little set of books on yellow pads just like Bill Lacy taught me. When our accounting team ran each month's financial statement, they were always amazed how close my yellow pad numbers were.

There is not a week that goes by that I don't have a meeting with our financial people. I always have a pulse on billings, profitability, projections, and collections. And, of course, how much cash is in the bank. Our T3 financial meetings take place on Friday afternoons as we wrap up another week. One Friday, I walked in the kitchen door at the ranch with a big grin on my face, and told my husband the company's cash balance. He said, "Maybe it is time to take the money and run off to Mexico." We haven't yet.

That knowledge drives my short-term gut decisions. All jokes aside, if things are looking good, I'm pretty quick to approve a new hire. If it is a little soft, we may kick that decision down the road. In either case, it is a fast decision based on years and years of financial knowledge. Cowgirls always know their numbers, whether it is their latest time barrel racing or their Q1 profit or loss. In fact, cowgirls live by the numbers.

A funny story: My husband started his career in the broadcasting business. He ran a radio station, and his credit policy was "cash in advance for politicians, preachers, and mobile home dealers." We all laugh and say that policy is still in effect today.

DON'T TOLERATE FINANCIAL MEDIOCRITY

I frequently meet female entrepreneurs who have tried to bootstrap their companies and far too often they confide in me that they have not paid themselves, sometimes for several years. They feel a need to appear to be more successful than they really are by paying their employees, but not themselves. My reaction is usually not good, probably because my mother also tried to appear more affluent than she really was almost all of her life.

Do not do this. Not paying yourself means you are not facing reality and that you are babying the business. Make a profit. If you cannot run in the black, then cut something out and make a profit, even if it is small in some years. Force yourself to make smart financial decisions quickly to ensure a profit. Do not allow your ego to drive you into financial mediocrity.

The same principle applies if you work for a company. You should receive a salary that is commensurate with the contribution you make. If you are engaged and productive and deserve a pay raise and a promotion, ask for it, but always be there with stats and numbers and results you have achieved.

We did a lot of work years ago in the area of pharmaceutical research where millions of dollars were spent on clinical research trials. They lived by one mantra, "fail fast." That meant that if a research project was going to fail, it was far better to do so early. Failing late in a trial meant tens of millions of dollars down the drain. When you have to cut your losses, you do it as soon as you can. Hanging on and not paying yourself is simply extending misery. I'm sure it has worked for some people. But I have much higher expectations of return on investments in both time and money.

Do not be afraid to apply a little creativity to finances. My accounting department has a long-standing policy of sending fresh-baked cookies to our clients' accounts payable team. A nice warm cookie has a way of putting your invoice on the top of the stack as one of the first to get paid.

BE A BIG CHARACTER

My father proclaimed there were more "characters per square inch" in Liberty, Texas, than any other place on earth. For example, there was "old man McGuire," who sat on his porch in the evening where he would pass on the wisdom of the ages to us kids. If I would say it was too hot, he would say, "Well, if it ain't cockroaches, it's bedbugs."

Guy Devore, the local grocer, had a famous trick of leaving a broom, package of cigarettes, or other items by the cash register. Without a blink, he would ring one of them up with a customer's other items. If you asked why, he would just say, "Oh, I thought it was yours."

The local jeweler was named Mr. Swindle.

Opal Hamilton, wife of the hardware store owner, wore a large picture frame hat, a mink stole, and white gloves to town every day well into her nineties.

Doc Griffin still made house calls.

When you become a powerful person, people pay attention. They talk about you and tell stories about you. That's just what people do. So think about those stories that your employees and colleagues tell behind your back and will never tell you about. If you provide them with good material, their stories about you will tend to be more complimentary and positive. A funny story about a character is always more interesting than something snarky.

I attended a big wedding in Dallas recently, and after the ceremony, the festivities moved out to the Dallas Country

Club (of course). I was with a friend and we came to the church in an Uber. We just needed a quick ride to the country club. I saw a big black Rolls-Royce go by, and I stopped and knocked on the window and asked if we could bum a ride. The driver looked a little shocked, but graciously agreed. When we got to the country club, another friend saw us drive up and said, "My God, Gay, do you know who was driving that car?" He told me that it was one of the wealthiest men in the United States, who rarely left home without a security detail. So I laughed and told everyone that I'd bummed a ride from a billionaire! My friends could not believe I had the gall.

We were in the Hamptons a few years ago at a media event and went out to dinner with our hosts. When we went into the restaurant, I saw Larry David sitting in a booth on the far side of the room and thought that was cool. We had a nice dinner and, as we started to leave, I saw that he was still there. My husband said, "Gay, don't do it." But I did and he watched in horror as I scooted up to Larry, sat down next to him in the booth, and said, "I never interrupt people like this, but my daughter loves you. Would you sign a napkin for her?" He replied, "Well, you did interrupt me, so what's her name?"

I admire characters. Texans like Herb Kelleher, Ann Richards, and Molly Ivins. Great people like Teddy Roosevelt and Winston Churchill. People talk about leaders. Stories become legendary. Give them some good material, a combination of awe-inspiring and funny is good. Be impulsive. Be a character.

DO UNEXPECTED, CRAZY THINGS

Part of being a character is doing unexpected, crazy things, and I have done my share of them. Again, opportunities come at you in strange ways if you put yourself out there. When you get opportunities to get out of your comfort zone, take them. Being bold and a little crazy empowers you.

- I've been on a coast guard cutter in the Falkland Islands.
- I've climbed the almost 14,000-foot-high Mount Kinabalu in Malaysia in the middle of the night.
- I've ridden in those giant dump trucks in coal mines in Wyoming.
- I have walked the Great Wall of China.
- I witnessed a pride of lions in Botswana stalk, kill, and eat a Cape buffalo. It took two hours.
- I attended a dinner in Latvia hosted by then-president Vaira Vīķe-Freiberga.
- I've driven a train—a private train, I might add.
- I once had a nice drink of Scotch served with ice from a million-year-old glacier in South America.
- I scratched the belly of an elephant seal sunning on a beach.
- I sang the French national anthem ("La Marseillaise") with drunk, off-duty *gendarmerie* on New Year's Eve in a café in Saint Martin.
- I swam to the edge of Victoria Falls in Africa, hung on for dear life, and felt a huge adrenaline rush!

Sure gives you a few good conversation starters. And it makes for good stories about you. Find your own path to becoming an interesting character.

NOTHING IS MORE POWERFUL THAN TRUST

Cowgirls win their horses' trust gradually, step by step. It takes time. It takes determination. It takes lots and lots of goodwill. If I have learned one thing in life, it is that building trust is the single most powerful thing you can do. If you earn someone's trust, you do it one step at a time until it forms a long-standing bond.

While climbing the enormous sand dunes in Namibia, I recall the voice of our guide. He said, "Step by step. Slow by slow." As I conjured every ounce of patience and strength I had, I eventually looked back and I had climbed the dune. It takes patience, extreme focus, and determination.

My business is built on trust. Our clients bet their careers that we will help them win. If we fail, they fail because they chose us. I failed a few times, but not many. When I did, I always raised my hand and took full responsibility for it. Sometimes I had to put my money where my mouth was, but I always tried to do the right thing.

Our obsession on winning client trust led us to many long-term client relationships—Dell was with us for over sixteen years. They trusted us to do what we said we would do, and we trusted them. That does not mean everything was easy, or a proverbial day at the beach. It did mean that problems could usually be resolved because everyone was working together in good faith. Both parties sought to find win-win resolutions.

Mutual trust speeds things up. When you have worked with someone for years and she tells you a project has been fully proofread, you simply accept her word for it. You don't need to check it for yourself. If we quote a price for a project for a long-standing client, they simply accept it because they know we will price it fairly for both parties.

An important caveat about trust: sometimes two parties trust each other too much. I have seen this happen when deadlines are short or a project's complexity spirals out of control. Sometimes, you get complacent that the other guy will save your ass one more time. I don't mind trying to save someone's ass, but when I move into ass-saving mode, it is my responsibility to let everyone know that risk has gone way up and ask the question, "Do you really need it that fast?" If the answer is yes, then we both must affirmatively acknowledge that together we are taking on more risk than normal. We have made that mistake more than once with the best of intentions. We teach our teams not to allow it.

Sometimes, years of trust can be compromised by a harsh word, terse e-mail, or an inappropriate text message. When this happens, apologize profusely, and if you have a legitimate concern, discuss it face-to-face and take responsibility. Try like hell to work things out and restore trust.

I remember my first trip to Corpus Christi after winning the Spohn Hospital account when I was introduced to the hospital CEO, Sister Kathleen Coughlin. Sister was very gracious to me and we had a good visit, talking about several pressing marketing projects to be addressed. When I got up to leave, she took my hand and said, "Remember, no money, no mission." I remember thinking what a smart woman she was; she had just made me feel responsible for the financial success of her heartfelt mission. She met me where I was, and I was hooked for life.

She could be alternately sweet, tough, demanding, and unpredictable. In the days before e-mail, she wielded voicemail like a sword, often leaving scathing messages for her staff in the middle of the night. She was a little unorthodox, but no one questioned her dedication toward her mission. I loved her dearly. Sister Kathleen was a cowgirl.

Stop for a moment and think about who trusts you blindly. Who do you trust? Go thank them.

SOMETIMES YOU HAVE TO PUSH YOURSELF

As athletes know, sometimes it is in the last ten yards of a run or exercise that you have to dig down deep and find that last burst of energy to carry you through. Cowgirls know this implicitly.

Recently, on the last day of an adventure-filled and physically challenging trip to Africa, I fell and broke my kneecap in half. I didn't know what I had actually done to my knee, but I did know I had to buck up and make the thirty-two-hour door-to-door trip home to Texas. With the help of wheelchairs and attentive British Airways flight attendants who diligently packed my knee in ice, I made it home. (Oh, and I did have a few gin and tonics along the way!)

However, my inspiration to keep going was one of my cowgirl heroines in this book, Fox Hastings. I kept thinking how Fox had broken her ribs in a rodeo but kept going and never quit, as if nothing had happened. She must have been in pain, as I was, but she kept a smile on her face, and the show went on. She said she could not let management and her fans down.

Many times in my life, my Rough Riders would tell me I was pushing myself too hard—to the point of sheer exhaustion. I can remember in my personal and business life sprinting the metaphorical last ten yards drawing on every bit of courage and energy I could muster. But, once again, like

Fox, I realized that people were counting on me. Family, employees, and clients. I simply did not want to let them down. So, in those times when I felt like I was hanging on by a thread, I tightened the girth and kept going.

The amazing thing about this is that you will many times miss out on the greatest things in your life and career if you don't push yourself past what you think you've got in you. Try it. You cannot sustain it every day, but the day will come when you need to reach out far and grab the prize. When others fail and fall behind, they will marvel at your courage. It is a great confidence builder and will set you apart from the herd!

YOUR GUT IS SMARTER THAN YOUR HEAD

I have been fortunate to have had many life experiences. Each experience is a lesson learned that gets filed away in your mind. Lesson upon lesson ultimately presents itself as gut feelings—instincts that help you navigate life. As those lessons become richer and more diverse, the better your instincts become. Your confidence builds, your character grows, and fear of failure diminishes.

Through the years we have had promising clients who were not performing up to our profitability standards. Sometimes we resigned them. But often, when we had a gut instinct that we could not only turn them around, but make them home runs, we loosened our standards and took a chance that we could make it work long-term. Those were always gut decisions. I remember clients that we nurtured for several years, making slow but steady progress. We were wrong about a couple of them, but most of those clients developed into major pieces of business for us.

One day I got a call from one of my account executives, who worked with Midland Memorial Hospital in Midland, Texas—one of our clients. She had just heard on the radio that an eighteen-month-old baby, named Jessica McClure, fell into a well in Midland and was stuck twenty-two feet below-ground. We knew that if the baby survived, she would end up at Midland Memorial Hospital. We immediately called our client to see if we could help but the phone lines were jammed. We decided that our only option was to hop on the next plane to Midland.

Our account executive was on-site in less than four hours. I would have gone as well, but I had a baby at home so I worked the phones from Austin. We did not wait to ask for permission from our client because we could not even find her; the two of us made the decision based on our gut instincts. Our client had a tiny staff and the look of relief on her face when my account executive arrived told the whole story. This was in the early days of CNN and "Jessica in the well" became a huge national television story. We were contracted to do advertising work for the hospital, not public relations. But our team, supported by writers and creative teams in Austin, worked with our client to manage the hospital newsroom and field interview requests from all over the world as rescue personnel tried to dig a parallel shaft to rescue Jessica. Some fifty-eight hours later they pulled her to safety on worldwide live television.

We stayed on the story from Midland and Austin for about a week fielding questions and wrapping up details. We never sent them a bill for any of our time or expenses. But we won the lifelong loyalty and trust from our clients, the hospital CEO, and the board of directors. It was simply the right thing to do. Almost thirty years later, if I need a reference for a new client, my call to Midland always gets returned within an hour or less.

Overall, I have had a great time in my business career, but I have also made some mistakes. A few really big ones. They almost all come down to decisions about who to hire or accept as a client. My last mistake was a doozy. I let someone into our company when my gut said no but my head insisted it was the logical thing to do. I learned my lesson, one more time, the hard way.

I can always tell when I do not like the choices before me, because I watch myself resisting making a decision. When we moved into our new Austin offices on Lamar Boulevard a few years ago, I hated all of the choices I saw for modular office furniture. It was too cube-like. I procrastinated and would not decide. Finally, Lee and our facilities manager started prototyping furniture we could build ourselves. It took a few iterations, but they got it right and I said yes the moment I saw it, and it has worked great.

Pay attention. Your gut is the unconscious network of all of your life experiences. It is everything you have learned about people, about success and failure. It does not explain itself; it presents no logical argument. You cannot run a search on it. Yet to ignore it almost always is a mistake. In fact, I cannot recall a time when my gut was wrong.

If you want to be powerful, when your gut and your head disagree, tell your head to shut up! Ride with your gut, especially the older you get. You will be right more often than not.

BRING ALONG SACKS OF HOPE, CHANGE, AND ENERGY WITH YOU

I walked into a bar in New York one afternoon after work to meet one of my clients. He was standing at the bar and said, "I just ordered a bottle of wine with a straw. What do you want?" He had had a rough day. So I pulled up a chair and listened. He was managing global marketing for a major pharmaceutical company and was beyond frustrated with how hard it was to implement change across such a huge organization. We did not find an answer that afternoon, but he was in a much better mood when we left because I listened to him vent.

Your customers want tangible results; that's the price of entry. But I have learned over the years that they want more. Many of our clients are in large organizations that are high-pressure environments often burdened by bureaucracy, complexity, and frequent management changes. If we can get them the results they need and then go one step further, we build powerful relationships. Clients often see us as change agents who can make their corporate lives better, or at least more fun. If we come in with creative concepts, a positive can-do attitude sprinkled with fun, and a few proactive big ideas, we make them smile and give them hope and energy. We actually can power them up to go back and effect positive change in their companies—which furthers their careers. And ours.

I have had so many clients tell me, "You are the highlight of my day. You come in upbeat with fresh ideas and challenge us with new thinking." We purposefully walk in with positive energy, excited by the work we are going to present, and it is so fun to see the smiles we leave behind.

We worked for a small nonprofit hospital in Temple, Texas, that remodeled their emergency room and wanted to attract more patient volume by becoming more of a walk-in clinic than a formal ER. This little hospital was literally across the street from one of the biggest, finest hospital systems in the country, Scott & White.

Great advertising campaigns are usually built upon a known belief, something that people believe is authentic and true. We did a few focus groups and found that Scott & White was notorious for long ER wait times. Everyone in the Temple area joked that Scott & White's "S&W" logo stood for "Sit & Wait." We seized on that insight and started a radio and television campaign that proclaimed our ER was for people who did not want to "Sit and Wait." The entire community got the joke, but what was so special was the impact it had on our client's staff. Their morale jumped because, for once, they stood tall and were able to best their very capable competitor. It was a huge emotional win for the entire organization, and the campaign won top national hospital marketing awards. Plus, we could measure the financial uptick from the ER visits and hospital stays coming from the ER. Just what I love, great creative that kicks ass and gets tangible financial results!

Done well, creating hope and energy yields another self-sustaining virtuous cycle that gets better and better over time. You gain power by understanding and creating that hope.

PRACTICE PROFOUND ACTS OF KINDNESS

Your clients and customers have career aspirations just like we all do. They have ambitions, egos, and dreams like us all. When you earn their trust, they begin to share some of those thoughts. When we were able to, we always tried to help make those dreams come true.

When Sister Kathleen, our client at Spohn Hospital, was elected president of the Texas Medical Association, I helped write her speech and produced her presentation for her. I made that wonderful lady look pretty hip. We had a client at Dell who was a great organizer and doer, but not very strategic. One of our senior account executives would meet with him over lunch once a month and help him brainstorm about his next moves. This guy understood that planning was not his strongest ability, and he genuinely appreciated our help. Focus on your strengths and get help with everything else.

We have worked on new ideas for good clients who were trying to sell an idea to their management teams. If a client had an idea and was trying to secure a budget to make it happen, we often would put together some concepts to support her or build some kind of prototype. We never charged for any of that work. We were always glad to help, and it always came back to us in spades. One of the most powerful things you can do for someone is give a hand without taking any of the credit.

Little things are so important. For years, when I handwrote all of those anniversary and birthday cards for all of our T3 team members, they were personal and filled with gratitude for their specific wonderful accomplishments. I reinforced in each card the good work recognized and rewarded at T3. I thanked our clients with real, genuine gratitude. My mother always told me that if you love someone and appreciate them, you should tell them. Right now.

A public act of profound kindness empowers us all. We recently had a six-year employee leave T3 to take a new job managing human relations at an Austin start-up—it was a remarkable opportunity for her and we all supported her decision. Her hometown is New Orleans. So after our last staff meeting that she would attend, one of her co-workers (who in a former career toured the world with Bob Marley and other reggae greats) stood up and started playing "When the Saints Go Marching In" on his trombone. Everyone got a white handkerchief and we had a parade around the office followed by beignets and rosé. It was a spontaneous outpouring of emotion, because she had touched every one of us during her years with us. She left T3 in tears of joy, feeling the respect and love that she earned.

OK, it was not spontaneous. It was planned down to the last detail by my wonderful Internal Development team, who deliver profound acts of kindness every day. They just made it look spontaneous! (Most companies have a Human Resources Department. At T3 we call it Internal Development because their primary focus is on growing and connecting our people.)

Lessons Learned: Cowgirls Use Competence to Find Confidence

- Confidence is earned, not awarded. After you have done all of the hard work to become competent, your expertise becomes the legitimate source of your confidence.
- You must build trust. Trust is the foundation of all relationships. I grew up with people who were far from wealthy, but their word made them richly respected. They never, ever let anyone down. They are my inspiration every day of my life.
- Oh, and never act desperate. People can smell it and will run away as fast as they can. Exude that confidence you have earned, and people will respect and follow you.

Prairie Rose Henderson
(Accession Number R.241.235 © Dickinson Research Center, National Cowboy & Western Heritage Museum, Oklahoma City, Oklahoma)

Chapter 7

COWGIRLS DESIGN THEIR OWN LIVES

One of my all-time favorite cowgirls is Prairie Rose Henderson. Her talent and fortitude earned her a place in the rodeos of the late 1800s when young horsewomen began competing against cowboys in a yearly gathering of cattle herds.

This progressed into the more organized rodeos. Prairie Rose was the exuberant daughter of a Wyoming rancher and decided one day she would ride to Cheyenne to enter a bronc busting contest. To her dismay, she was told she could not ride in the contest because she was a woman. She demanded to see the rules and found there was nothing stating that women could not participate. The officials had to let her compete.

I can only imagine what a stir this created when Prairie Rose came crashing out of the chute. Women and men alike were shocked and amazed. She didn't win that day, but I guess she really did. By not taking no for an answer, she won the right for women to compete in rodeos.

Eventually she did have many wins at the rodeos. She was known as the most flamboyant and creative cowgirl of her time. Wearing bloomers that she designed, sometimes hemmed in ostrich feathers, and vests covered with bright sequins, she stole the show.

In 1932, Prairie Rose was on her way to a competition and got caught in a blizzard. Nine years later her body was discovered, and the only way they identified her was by her champion belt buckle. Even in death, she was a winner and triumphed by living her life her way. After all, cowgirls design their own lives.

Designing your life is about deciding who you want to be. Today, in five years, in twenty years. In my view, a well-lived life means becoming a powerful woman to enable you to do the things you both need and want to do for yourself, your family, and others. Find that personal power and you can, to a large extent, design your own life—a life that will be very different as you move through the natural cycles we all face. If you don't do it, someone else will.

Cowgirls grow up with a realistic view of life. They see beloved old dogs die. They see the miracle of baby goats. They experience both wonder and tragedy and meet both head-on. *Cowgirls understand that there are some things they can control and other things they cannot.* They put all their energy on the things they can control.

IT IS NOT ABOUT WORK-LIFE BALANCE. IT IS ABOUT LIFE.

I have always been a driven person and I instinctively forge ahead on multiple fronts. I am often unsure of exactly where I am going, but I feel I am following a path, moving in a good direction, and am excited about what might reveal itself around the next curve. Embrace the world. You can have a new style of living and working that is fluid. You can work anywhere. Shop online. Work at home. Stay connected to work, kids, husband, and family. Focus on what matters right now. Is it finishing your white paper? Or looking over your son's book report?

The work–life question implies that one is bad and one is good. That is not true. If you think of it that way, you are going to mess it up. It is all the same thing. It is all important. That is, if you love what you do. If you don't love what you do, you will never find any balance. Walk away. Your glass will always be half-empty. But, as a Facebook friend once posted, "If you think your glass is half-empty, quit bitching and pour it in a smaller glass."

When I told my co-workers in 1983 that I was pregnant with my daughter, Rebecca, they were happy for me, but the inevitable question quickly came up: Would I come back to work after she was born? Looking back at this point in my life, I never let myself think about not coming back to work. I knew that I had to have my own independent source of income to help support my mother financially. I put my head down and decided to build the very best team, who could cover for me during my maternity leave. As the months progressed, my client portfolio grew substantially. I had one of the biggest, most profitable group of accounts at the company.

I scheduled a meeting with our president and presented him with my baby plan. I showed him how my accounts had grown over the past year. I explained what I had done to build up my team both at the office and at home. I told him that I planned to take two months off and then come back to work, but just working a half day for nine months. Before he could react, I said, "But even if I am in the delivery room having the baby, I will take care of things and we won't miss a beat." It was a powerful performance! He said OK. He knew I had him over a barrel.

I had a college student help me with Rebecca. My mother decided to move to Austin from Liberty to help me. Mother took a job teaching at a preschool and took care of Rebecca most afternoons.

LET'S DISPENSE WITH THE GUILT

Running my own business gave me a lot of flexibility around attending the children's school and extracurricular events. I was pretty good about showing up and would move mountains to do so. However, I will never forget one time that I couldn't show up. It was when Rebecca was in the third grade, and she was one of the stars of the Japanese play her teacher produced. I had an out-of-town meeting that was critical to the success and future budget of one of my hospital accounts. There was just no way I could get back in time for the play.

My mother stepped in. And, I mean *really* stepped in! She took Rebecca to her hairdresser and had Rebecca's long hair put up in a lovely twist with flowers worked in. She made sure Rebecca's costume was perfect, and that her makeup looked authentic and spot-on. She also photographed the event. All of this sounds great, right? It would have been, but I never heard the end of it.

My mother threw it up to me over and over through the years, of how I missed an important event in the young life of my precious daughter. Guilt, guilt, and more guilt heaped on. I always got a pang in my stomach when the topic of "The" Japanese play came up. Oh, and to top it off, my mother framed one of the beautiful photos of Rebecca in a lovely, ornate sterling silver frame. It is still on my dresser at the ranch as an ongoing reminder of my guilt.

We kept that hospital account for many years, and the budget grew and grew each year! I am also quite sure that account helped to pay for Rebecca's most expensive pastime—riding and showing her Arabian horse, Shesa. I drove her out to her riding lessons as much as I could, and I was always amazed at how strict and demanding her trainer, Martha, was with her. Rebecca never complained, not once. By the way, Rebecca is a cowgirl.

Oh, and cowgirls don't let guilt get in the way of long-term success. Cowgirls say bullshit to someone heaping on guilt, and move on—unless it's your mother!

TOO MANY DOGGONE DOGS

As if things were not complicated enough, I was always rescuing dogs. Some from the grip of death. We usually had four or five large dogs running through the house, riding in the back of the Suburban on trips to the ranch. One even became a medical miracle, our beloved Joe David. I found him abandoned on the side of the road to our Double Heart Ranch. I loaded him in the truck, and my mind started racing about how I would convince Lee to let me keep him. I already had a herd of dogs that were pretty annoying. When I drove up to the ranch house, Lee was standing with his hands on his hips, shaking his head. I swear I don't know where this came from, but I jumped out and said, "Look, Lee, it's little Joe David!" Joe David was the name of our small-town local banker. Lee laughed at the name, and I knew I had saved another dog. The name was actually appropriate because we soon learned that the dog had the same view on life that our banker friend did—affable, friendly, trusting, and laid-back.

THE BABIES ARE COMING. THE BABIES ARE COMING.

Running your own business is full of risk and challenges. But it also gives you an awesome ability to design your own life. I have the flexibility to walk away from a piece of business that is not a good fit for us—either for cultural, strategic, or financial reasons. Each time I make one of those calls I gain a little more respect from my staff because they know I have our collective best interest at heart.

A few years after I got my company up and running, four of my twenty-four employees got pregnant. How they all got pregnant at close to the same time, I'll never know. We must have had an ice storm that year. Of course, I was thrilled for them but then started lying awake at night worrying about how we were going to manage through their maternity leave and whether they would want to return to work. We had some very candid conversations about it. The moms-to-be assured me they wanted to continue to work if they could find good childcare for their babies, although I knew two of them came from well-to-do families and did not have to work.

After thinking about it for a few days, I realized that we did not have to play by anyone else's rules—we were in control of our own destiny. So I proposed that after their maternity leave they bring the babies to the office to hang out with us until they started to crawl and/or walk. None of us was sure this would work, but we all agreed to try it. We also agreed that this was not my company providing day care. The babies were the responsibility of their moms. We never drew up any contracts, waivers, or anything like that. We just did it because I thought it was the right thing to do.

One of the moms backed out at the last minute, gave back her maternity leave check, and said she could not do it. We convinced her to give it a try and it worked out beautifully. In fact, she and one of the other first moms ended up starting their own company together. Their children are the closest of friends today.

We started with two little ones, then within weeks two more. It was a bit daunting at first, but we all quickly got into a groove. If a baby cried, whoever was not on the phone grabbed it and waltzed it around the office. When they were asleep, we worked like fiends. We all laughed and said this is what growing up on a family farm must have been like, and it was. Everyone pitched in. The babies thrived and loved the experience. They were outgoing and fun. Our clients loved to stop in and say hi, so did our mailman and all our suppliers who were in and out of the office daily. The babies made everyone smile every day. (Paul, the mailman that we had for twenty-something years, sent me flowers when he retired. He loved being greeted so warmly each day at T3.)

People were amazed that we could actually work with babies around the office. But we did, the babies were fine, the moms were fine, and the business grew because of the quality of the work we were doing. A lot of that quality came from the emotional bonds we built among each other. This was where I learned about the power of trust between team members. We formed bonds that are still there, almost thirty years later.

We named the program T3 & Under, and it has been in place since 1995. It is the single most powerful thing I have done in my life. What we have done for the families of our employees is nothing short of remarkable. And, when I say "we," I mean everyone at T3. There is not one employee in the company who has not smiled at a baby, opened the door for a mom, or carried a car seat to a car. It is a very tight team that absolutely loves and trusts each other.

I have been honored for T3 & Under at the White House. I've been on the *Today Show* twice and ABC's *Nightline*, featured in *USA Today* and Bloomberg TV, visited by the US Department of Labor, and have had hundreds of other articles published about the success of the program. Our case has been cited in several books. The impact on the company has been transformative and sustainable. And, by the way, we do have a formal policy in place these days.

Not long after we began hosting babies at work, one of our developers came up to me and said that he did not have a baby, but he did have a dog and asked if he could bring his dog to work from time to time. I said OK, we would try it. We have had hundreds of dogs in the office over the years with virtually no problems. They all have to be on flea control, be perfectly housebroken, and cannot be aggressive. A few times we had a code yellow or code brown alert, but this usually was for puppies who had to go home until they could learn to contain themselves. The dogs love coming to work and playing with each other every day. Patting a friendly dog on the head can take such pressure off of a stressful deadline.

I had a production artist whose daughter was raising a little goat for a 4-H project. The goat was on medication and needed pills several times a day, so she brought it to work for a few days to take care of it. She kept it in a little box under her desk. I thought, no big deal, that's fine. But the next week we had a major infestation of fleas. Fleas were everywhere. It was gross. So, making another power play, I announced a firm NO GOAT policy that stands today.

As of September 2017, we have had over one hundred babies. We will have had several more by the time this book is published. Most of the babies come with their moms, but several fathers have brought their children because their wives worked in situations where a baby at work was not possible. One wife was an expert Mercedes-Benz mechanic, so the dad brought their baby to T3 & Under.

One dad who brought two little girls over the years to T3 & Under told me recently what an impact those months of caring for his children had made in his relationship with them as they grew up. He recently left T3 to accept a huge, career-making opportunity, and we were all thrilled for him. His departure was one of the most emotional ones in the history of the company, not least because he had earned the love and respect of every employee at T3 for the way he manned up and took care of those little girls.

Over the years, T3 & Under has created this amazing network of parents and children. If you help care for someone's baby, guess who gets invited to a birthday party or to join a little league team? We have events throughout the year, like Halloween, where we invite the kids who have been through the program to come back. It is so fun to see them grow up and have this special relationship with each other. Parents exchange information on everything from pediatricians to remodeling contractors on a daily basis.

Today, "Moms of T3" is one of the most popular channels on our Slack messaging application. It links moms in four cities across the country. A quick question about a day care facility or a good family doctor gets almost immediate responses. One of our working moms did a post about a company named Milk Stork. They provide special packaging for moms traveling for business to safely ship breast milk home via overnight delivery. I approved this service as a reimbursable expense within a day of learning about it.

By the way, our staff decided to change the name of the Slack channel from "Moms of T3" to "Parents of T3." Now we have dads right in the middle of the dialogue, and that makes it an even more powerful tool for our families.

In the summer of 2016, both of those first two T3 & Under babies were back at work at T3 as college interns. Both will have a leg up once they enter the job market by having the T3 internship experience on their résumé. Life comes full circle. By the way, our internship program has grown into a highly coveted experience. This year, on the first day we posted openings for our 2017 summer program we received over five hundred applications. Before it was over, we had two thousand applications.

When I am asked about the rewards of owning your own business, I always say that nothing makes me prouder than the quality of our people and the quality of the work they do. I am so proud of the jobs we have created and the families we have supported. A good job is a path to dignity, self-satisfaction, and an interesting life. We have helped people connect, helped build their networks and thrive. We have supported our clients and helped them succeed. I have called my own shots for a long time. No matter what happens in the future, no one can take those successes away from me.

WHO TAKES CARE OF THE KIDS?

I get questions about how two hard-charging, career-focused people can manage the work–life balance thing every time I speak. I have seen all kinds of creative solutions and some pretty dramatic failures. The best way to deal with this is to get the ego and emotion out of the conversation and to make a good business decision for the good of the family. Do you have the resources and support to enable you both to actively pursue a rewarding career? If you are both high-income people, the answer is probably yes. Even though childcare is expensive, it is probably a great investment when you calculate the value of two long-term salaries if you both stay in the workforce.

If one of you has significantly higher earning potential in a gratifying career than the other, then that one should probably pursue a career and the other should focus on the kids, regardless of who is male or female. I have seen many successful women with husbands who have taken the lead raising the children and made their own careers a second priority. Based on my personal experience, this is especially true of women who make it into the C-suite and take high-paid, powerful, high-pressure positions. I admire these men immensely— just as I admire women who have put their husband's career ahead of their own for the benefit of the entire family. Most of these men are in careers such as teaching that they can do on a part-time basis and come back to when the kids are older. Make a good business decision that is in everyone's best interest. Times like these separate the men from the boys. Or the cowgirls from the girls.

Remember Annie Oakley and Frank Butler. Frank was the star of the show until one day Annie stepped on the stage. Suddenly, Annie became the show and, ultimately, a superstar. The two of them worked it out and made a good business decision. Annie performed and Frank became her manager. Together, they were a huge success because each was focused on what they did best, and they totally trusted each other. They were married for fifty-plus years. After she died, he was devastated and stopped eating. He died eighteen days later.

Most of our team members at T3 are fairly young and either single or married and just starting their families. Almost all of those families have two working professionals who share responsibilities for the kids. Things go back and forth, and yes, moms probably do more. But the good news is that the dads are certainly in the game and very involved in their families. I see this new generation of men taking a much more active role in raising their kids, which I think is a great thing.

It is so important for working married couples to take a real interest in each other's careers. If you do not understand what is going on with your spouse's career, it is hard to understand when to give and not give. Don't leave work at work. Bring it home, talk about it, and build mutual empathy. Understand the challenges and opportunities. If you take the time and show a genuine interest, when a big decision about careers comes your way you will not be blindsided. You will be prepared and your gut instinct will be good. My experience is that if you aren't taking an interest in each other's careers, someone else at work will fill that role and be a confidant.

TIMELINE YOUR LIFE

I strongly recommend that families, but especially women, sit down and do a lifetime timeline. Here's why. Most women I know are pretty selfless when they have kids. They are in the moment with their families and rarely think about their careers after the kids grow up. I have seen it over and over again, with young mothers making decisions about their careers and childcare with little, if any, real consideration of the long-term consequences to their family finances, their lifelong careers, and the overall opportunities for the collective family.

So stop and take the time to think about how old your kids will be in five years. How old you and your partner will be. How about in ten? Or fifteen? Of course, we cannot be certain of the future, but we can anticipate the big, likely events such as high school, college, first jobs, empty nests, and aging parents. Those big buckets are pretty easy to figure out. Then think about your goals and your dreams and see where they fit on your timeline. It gets pretty interesting pretty quick.

We all get swept up in the moment, and it's hard to stop and take stock. Ask yourself: Where is my life right now, and where do I want it to go? Sure, the kids are a priority right now. But what can I do right now to improve my chances of hitting a career home run when the kids are gone? Little steps here and there can add up to huge advantages later in life.

Go back through your timeline and think about money. What will childcare cost? College? What are the family's priorities? Sketch it out. Look for options. Have those important, fierce conversations. Deal with the short term. Think about long-term earning potential. Share it with your spouse. Have a healthy debate. Explore ideas. Get on the same page.

Then share it with your kids. Explain that the timeline is not about certainty, but is about defining directions you would like to explore. Put some of their ideas into the timeline and give them the gift of having a sense of the family's goals, values, and dreams. Believe me, it will be a true gift. And, as opportunities come up along the way, you all will be much quicker to connect the dots on which ones are most important.

I know a powerful woman who was chief operating officer of a major public company. She had been incredibly successful, but had a desire to move into a chief executive officer role, and that passion would just not go away. When she got a chance, she took it. It required a move across the country and a change in her husband's job. I sat with her in her office one afternoon and heard her dealing with her junior-high-aged daughter, who was traumatized about being taken away from her friends because of the move. Her son also went through lots of turmoil and short-term anxiety.

I was so proud of her because she owned all of those issues. She took responsibility for it all and believed with her whole heart that even though it meant a big change for them, it was the right thing to do for everyone. Had she not taken the position, it would have been a lifelong regret. She did her timeline, understood the issues and, happily, it has worked out. Her family has thrived and she has grown as an executive. Her husband has successfully restarted his career. She earned her family's respect for making what they now understand was the right call. She's one brave cowgirl.

TAKE AIM ON WHAT MATTERS

Life comes at you in terrible ways sometimes. The husband of one of my best friends was killed in an aviation accident. He was young, vibrant, funny. He was there one day, and then he wasn't. I was having lunch with her when we got the call.

I dropped everything, canceled every meeting, and moved into her house and appointed myself interim COO. The house was full of mourners and people who loved them both. They told stories about him and wished her well and shared her sadness. I sat in his empty office, worked the phones, and ran the household for a week. No one asked me to do it. No one questioned my authority to do it. It mattered to me very much to take the lead for a few days and let her grieve. And it was the best way for me to grieve as well.

In January 2009, when we came back from the Christmas holidays, the country was in real financial trouble. Major institutions were on edge, the markets went south, and everyone was in near panic. I started to get bad phone calls. Our clients started cutting their budgets. They were very apologetic and assured us it was no reflection on our work. They were being forced to make cuts across the board. Some of our vendors were not able to fulfill contracts because of lack of inventory. We went into emergency mode with twice-daily briefings. We focused on keeping our very best people. We focused on doing more with less, everywhere. It was one of the most brutal experiences I have ever had because it was totally out of our control. I was always used to being able to pull a few levers here and there to make things better. This time, there were not any levers that made things better. Sometimes none of your choices are good ones. Sometimes it doesn't rain and there is not a damn thing you can do about it.

This is where reality kicks in. We did not hide or bury our heads in the sand. We owned the problem and worked it every day. We were forced to make tough decisions about who should stay and who should go, and what things we could cut that were nice but not necessary. People got their feelings hurt, and some got mad and said unkind things about me, but I never let it bother me because there were so many who hugged me and thanked me for the opportunity to work at T3. I understand the emotions and the fear. We all face challenges. Your character is defined by how you handle them. Both in this moment and in thinking back, I see that my grit was reflected in my staff. I wasn't in it alone: They were in it with me. Many took salary cuts. All applied extra effort, time, and creativity to see us all through. I won't take credit for their positivity and perseverance as they powered through. But damn, I was proud!

It took us two years to recover, and we were one of the

lucky ones because our digital roots saved us. We were doing programs that had tangible, proven results. In a sea of uncertainty, our clients started shifting budgets to programs that could prove success. As those budgets began to move from traditional advertising toward digital, we caught an uplift that turned the business in a better direction. Many were less fortunate than we were.

YOU CAN DO BOTH AT THE SAME TIME

My daughter, Rebecca, went with me on a Committee of 200 trip to China. When I was speaking to the young women students in Beijing, they had lots of questions for me. One of them asked Rebecca, who was sitting in the audience, about what it was like growing up with a working mother. I took a deep breath, because I had never talked to Rebecca about this. I had no idea what she would say. Rebecca did not hesitate. She said, "There were a lot of times when my mom was not there and I missed her, but I remember that when she was there, she was all there. I knew she loved me and I was fine. And how many daughters get to go to China with their moms? We would not be here with you today if she did not have her career."

With all the distractions that come at us today it is important to be mindful of being present in the moment—both for parents and children. If you learn to manage the flow between work and family life, you can absolutely deal with work and family needs at the same time. Just understand that often, priorities can change multiple times within the course of one day. Of course it can be stressful, but don't let it be surprising. Build a support system.

Start with your boss, then your team, then friends and family—oh, and then your partner or husband! Prepare them, build contingencies, run it like a military operation. Always have an emergency bag handy filled with snacks, wipes, towels, toys, books, Band-Aids and more. Practice reciprocity among friends, co-workers, and neighbors. We always took care of each other's kids as neighbors in Austin, Texas. One of Rebecca's little three-year-old girlfriends took a bath with her almost every night, and Lee carried her home in her pj's. She was hiding out from her two rowdy older brothers.

Our son Ben was recently holding his one-year-old daughter, standing in line waiting for a taco he ordered. Suddenly, she threw up all over him and the floor of the restaurant. The restaurant people ran to help clean things up; Ben wiped his shirt off as best he could. He stood there smelling of baby spit-up but still focused on getting his taco. Manage the priorities, choose the more important focus, and clean up the resulting mess as soon as you can. He got his taco.

RUN IT LIKE THE FAMILY FARM—EVERYONE PITCHES IN

Cowgirls were traditionally raised on the family farm or ranch, where everyone pitched in with everything from daily chores to rounding up cattle to baling hay. Everyone, except the smallest children, was expected to help. And, in that process, everyone understood the realities of running the family business. The kids saw the good, the bad, and the ugly.

I know a woman who is an amazing lawyer, and she started taking her kids to the law firm on Sunday afternoons so she could catch up on work. No one could be offended by them being there on a Sunday. She took great care to give them things to do, show them where the bathrooms were, areas where they could quietly hang out. Her kids were so well be-haved that she started bringing them on school holidays or bad weather days. No one could object because the kids were not a problem. She made partner. The kids did great, and all of them won the respect of everyone at the law firm.

Even though you may work in an office tower, miles away from your home, it is important to let your children know about what is going on at work. Of course, their ability to un-derstand will depend on their age. But if you had a hard day at work, you need to be honest with them. If you are not can-did with them, they will still pick up your emotional stress but not know what to do about it. Or whether they caused it. If it is clear your stress comes from outside the home and family, then their energy can be channeled into helping with dinner or finding a way to be silly and make you laugh.

One of our kids liked to put on my high school clown cos-tume and run around the neighborhood. One thought she was a cheetah and ran up and down the hall on all fours. And one did the herky-jerky dance on cue. If that doesn't cheer you up, nothing will!

And don't forget to share the good with the kids. One of our team leaders makes a point to share big successes at work with her kids. They don't really need to completely un-derstand everything. Simply knowing that something good happened to Mommy is powerful. Especially if it means ice cream for them. Share your experiences at work to show them how you help people. Show them how ideas come together. Show them your creativity and curiosity. Teach them to argue from two sides of an issue. Show them your innovation. Take them to work, invite their friends, book a conference room, and let them have a meeting. Teach them PowerPoint. Teach them to work together using sticky notes and voting on the best ideas. Take your talent to their school. Show your leadership. Invite your clients to a birthday party. Teaching your kids about your work and sharing some fun, new things creates buckets of goodwill that go miles and miles when things get challenging.

Be inspiring to your kids by letting them see this side of you. It can make a tremendous difference in their perspective on life and will make them more well-rounded people. You and your kids will be more powerful.

ASKING FOR HELP INDICATES REAL HONESTY

For years I prided myself on doing it all. We had kids in grade school, a growing company, and I had a lot of volunteer obligations. I had lunch with a friend one day and confided in her that I was on the edge of burning out. She told me to hire a personal assistant. I resisted because no one else at T3 had a personal assistant. But I listened to her and, again, worked through my guilt.

The job description we wrote was simple—that my assistant's responsibility was to give me time back. Anything that she could do to give me time back was a win. I only had two priorities—the kids and building the company. She took the dry cleaning, went shopping, took the dogs to the vet, managed the calendar, set up meetings, made travel arrangements, and found gifts for clients. I used to write every check to pay every bill at home and at the office. She found someone to help do all of that. At first, I worried that it might be beneath her to deal with things like dry cleaning. But an interesting thing happened. She won the respect of everyone in the organization because she completely understood her job. Because she did so much, I was able to spend more time in front of clients, which ultimately is always a good financial move for your business. Our staff saw the benefits of that and gave her all the credit. She made me so much more effective by helping me focus on what really mattered, and what only I could do to drive T3 forward.

If you are advancing your career and raising a family, you have to have help. Trying to do it all will simply wear you out. Exhaustion does not produce power. Be strategic, think it through, be creative—ask for help. Don't let the cost of help be an obstacle. Build the cost of help into your business plan. One or two new business successes or raises can be more than enough to cover the costs.

Be brutally honest about what you need. Think about next month, next year, and the next ten years. Not asking for help is the single most dangerous thing you can do for you, your family, and your career. And it will make people who actually can help you feel good about themselves. We know from history that cowgirls helped each other and took care of each other's children. What are the possibilities? Think about sharing a nanny. Think about moving willing grandparents closer. Think about working from home part of the time. Or team up with some co-workers to find a great solution. Believe me, I know it is not easy. But do be creative. If you practice reciprocity and help each other out, you will find your power.

STAY IN THE GAME

I have a few female friends who graduated with college degrees, married into money, and then dropped their careers to take care of their kids. These were capable, talented women. A few of them ended up in painful divorces. Today the kids are gone. These women are in their fifties, have no business credentials at all and very little income. It is OK to step back from a promising career for a while, but never get completely out. My friends will tell you, staying in the game in some way will give you lots of options.

I have a talented woman who has worked with me for years. While she was raising young children, her mother's health took a dramatic turn for the worse. She tried to manage it all, but it got to be too much and she quit. But she maintained her amazing network of people. She made a point of having power lunches several times a month to maintain close personal relationships. She told people the truth about her struggles, but stayed informed about industry changes. She eventually came back with a vengeance and a better understanding of what matters to her, and what could be a win for T3.

Raising a family is a long-term undertaking. Don't let short-term emotions control your decisions. We all have times in our lives when we need to take a break. It has happened twice to me. First, when I was pregnant with my daughter, Rebecca, and then much later in life, when my mother went through a dramatic bad turn with her health. When I had Rebecca, I was working for someone else. When my mom needed me, I was self-employed. I was thankful both times I was able to do what mattered.

One important point. I discussed earlier the power of doing something you love. Women who are not happy at work tend to think about opting out when they do not believe their circumstances will improve at work. If they are not challenged and empowered to grow themselves or others, they are less likely to put in the effort to make it work. Some of my powerful female friends think that too many women "hide behind" the needs of their children to avoid conflict and pressure in high-pressure jobs. I know women who have gone through medical school, opened successful practices, and bailed out to focus on their kids. I tend to think that many of these women worked in environments that they did not love or had supervisors they did not respect.

Put doing something you love high on your list for a successful life. People who love what they do find ways to make it work. This is why knowing yourself is so important. You can then read the tea leaves and begin to understand what you truly love and what you are truly good at.

Another option that I have seen work is going back to school. No one will fault you for furthering your education. Getting an MBA can be very powerful. Go for certifications. Learn to code. Actively participate in a community of learning. Be curious.

NEGOTIATE WIN-WIN

I talk about buckets of goodwill. You make deposits into those buckets by the way you treat people. By being responsible, trustworthy, and brave.

One of my most trusted, loyal team members came to me one day with tears in her eyes and told me that her sister had been diagnosed with terminal cancer and she only had a few months to live. She told me that her family had decided to care for her sister themselves and asked if she could take a leave of absence to care for her. No one in my organization owned more goodwill. My response was "You go do what you need to do. Stay in your job at full salary, watch the big stuff from home. Delegate everything else." Her staff at work pitched in and worked extra hours to help her. It was a terrible thing for her family to go through. But they were there, all in. We never experienced one problem in the months she was gone because even though she was not physically there, she watched everything like a hawk. She is back now, hard at work, and we both grew from this experience because we both did the right thing.

Pretty much all of the women who work at T3 are cowgirls. If they are not when they arrive, they learn the values pretty quickly. When they need some time off, or a raise or a promotion or all of the above, I watch closely because I remember doing the same thing years ago. The first thing they do is to ask for advice. They check in with our Internal Development department, with a few peers and a few of our long-time employees. Then they begin to build a case to justify it. Once they have thought it through, they go out and build support among their teammates. If it is a maternity leave request, they already have their support network built to help cover their time off. I have had many of them come tell me they were pregnant and then pull out their computer and walk me through a presentation about how they were going to manage it. I have rarely, if ever, seen them come in with unreasonable demands. They tend to be very thoughtful and do an admirable balancing act between their self-interest and the company's best interest. They usually get what they want. When dealing with work and family issues, be expansive in your ideation. Don't go with the most obvious, easy ask. Think it through. Be strategic. Go stand on both sides of the issue.

Another tamale story on tough negotiations: When I served on the board of directors for the Lower Colorado River Authority, the directors got to know each other pretty well, and would exchange personal and humorous stories during the breaks in our meetings. One story was told by a prestigious Texas businessman who, among other things, owned a popular Mexican restaurant in South Texas. He recalled that many years ago an elderly lady in a buttoned-up powder-blue wool suit, simple white cotton gloves, matching blue rhinestone earrings, and a pillbox hat walked into his restaurant late in the afternoon of Christmas Eve. The restaurant was crowded because they made the best tamales in town, and tamales are the traditional Christmas Eve meal. She waited in line and finally got to the counter. (My board friend happened to be working in his restaurant that afternoon because they needed the help and he enjoyed greeting so many of his loyal customers.) She looked him in the eye and said, "I'll have three tamales—one beef and two pork, and I'll have them wrapped up in a paper bag with three napkins." My friend responded, "I'm so sorry, but we are sold out of tamales; these people put their orders in days ago." She didn't budge and looked directly at him and said, "I told you, I want three tamales—one beef and two pork, and I'll have them wrapped up in a paper bag with three napkins." Once again, he said they were sold out. Suddenly, she reached over the counter and grabbed him by the collar and shook her finger in his face and said, "Look, you little son of a bitch, I'll have three tamales—one beef and two pork, and I want them wrapped up in a paper bag with three napkins and I want them right now!"

She walked out with three tamales—one beef and two pork in a paper bag with three napkins. I am not suggesting you negotiate like this lady, but I am suggesting you have some of her strength, tenacity, and conviction. After all, she was a widow who lived all alone, and the tamales meant a lot to her and her family in the past as a Christmas tradition. So sometimes you just cannot take no for an answer. Even in that pillbox hat, that lady was a cowgirl.

CHILDREN BENEFIT FROM WORKING PARENTS

I have always been a working mom, so that is the only perspective I have. It has often been tough, but as I look back on it, there have been many benefits, just as I'm sure there are for moms who have chosen to stay at home. My mother was a big believer in exposing children to the arts, galleries and museums, and interesting experiences early and throughout their childhood. As a first-grade teacher, she taught thousands of children to read through the years. She knew that reading to children from infancy could be terribly important to their development and later success in school.

When I first started my business, we were strapped for cash. Many times I had to tell the kids that they couldn't have something they wanted, because we just could not afford it. Early on, instead of lavish vacations and indulging them with material things, we would create fun out in the country at my godfather's farm or at the South Texas ranch. Lee's mother had an area in her yard that was designated as the children's mudhole. She let them turn on the garden hose and gave them tin cups and cupcake pans and just let them play. They entertained themselves for hours, delighted with the unique experience of being covered in mud. On rainy days, we would go to a grocery store, pick up some discarded cardboard boxes, and make spaceships or castles out of them in our living room. The kids still talk about all the wonderful things we built together.

Powerful, successful parents provide huge opportunities to

their children—don't underestimate the upside. Harvard Business School professor Kathleen McGinn co-authored a new study of fifty thousand adults in twenty-five countries. The study concluded that daughters of working mothers completed more years of education, were more likely to be employed and in supervisory roles, and earned higher incomes. Professor McGinn said, "Part of this working mothers' guilt has been, 'Oh, my kids are going to be so much better off if I stay home,' but what we're finding in adult outcomes is kids will be so much better off if women spend some time at work."[13]

I had lunch recently with a very senior woman in a leading technology company. I asked her about her career and how it had impacted her children. She said she would not do anything different because, as her children started their own careers, she became their coach and valued advisor. They respected her knowledge of the business world because she had proven herself there for so many years. She told me that the bonds between herself and her children had become stronger as they matured.

One of my serial entrepreneur friends also enjoys investing in promising new companies that are using technology to solve real-life problems. I found out he has an interesting technique for evaluating whether or not he wants to invest. First of all, you have to prepare your presentation for him. It has to be succinct, polished, and reveal a business plan where the numbers work. However, here is the deal: If you ask him to listen to your pitch, you must not only present to him, but also to his wife and their nine-year-old daughter. One entrepreneur told me that he went through this process and the kid was the one who scared him the most! What a wise and interesting approach. It is truly a family investment, and how wonderful it is for a young girl to be asked her opinion and listen to indi-viduals pitching their ideas and dreams. Powerful stuff.

Parents with interesting careers can create amazing op-portunities for their kids. My daughter-in-law, Morgan, grew up in a family business that customized specialty trucks and manufactured heavy equipment trailers. She started attending trade shows as a little girl. When she learned to drive, she started delivering dump trucks and water trucks to clients all over Texas because her parents knew she was responsible and they trusted her implicitly. Plus, having a bright, knowledge-able teenage girl drive up in their new water truck made a big impression on the buyers. A cowgirl for sure.

I have a friend who invites me to have coffee with his junior-high-aged daughter about twice a year. He goes out of his way to give her several opportunities a month to have adult conversations with interesting people. There is no agenda, and the conversation goes where the conversation goes. But I promise you it works. She is one of the most self-confident, in-teresting young women I have met in a long time and she is already a cowgirl.

One day, I was leaving for the office for an early meeting. As I got in my car and backed out of the driveway, I saw my two-year-old, Rebecca, standing in the bay window scream-ing and crying as I drove off. I thought I was going to die. As soon as I got to the office (this was before the days of cell phones), I called the babysitter and hoped she was consoling Rebecca. She laughed and said, "As soon as you were out of sight, Rebecca ran in the kitchen, munched on Cheerios, and started laughing and playing with her toys." Out of sight. Out of mind.

MAKE YOUR OWN LUCK

There are things that you can control in designing your own life. There are things you cannot control, and then there are serendipitous things that lie somewhere in the middle. These are the things that you do that radically increase your odds of having good luck.

In 2004, one of my major clients invited me to join her on a business outreach trip to Latvia. It was an opportunity for businesswomen in the United States to meet and share some of our experiences with businesswomen in the Baltic states. I agreed to go because I was flattered to be invited and excited to spend some quality time with a client I admired for her success and magnetic good nature. I really had no expectations for the trip other than that.

Once there I engaged to the best of my ability. I reached out to everyone I met and tried to meet them where they were. And many of them were in amazing, powerful positions. I met Bonnie McElveen-Hunter, the former ambassador to Finland, who was running the Red Cross at the time. I also met Denise Morrison, Nancy Peterson Hearn, Lynn Utter, Cordia Harrington, and Carolee Friedlander, who were active in C200. A few weeks after I got back, I got a letter asking me if I would like to apply for membership in C200. I did and it changed my life.

We each make our own luck by doing things that open us up for the potential to have good luck. If I had not taken that one trip, my life would have turned out very different. Success is not a straight line from point A to point B to point C. Think of it more like a pinball machine. You play hard and fast—you bounce around a lot. You are open and competent. You meet a lot of people, build a powerful network. You recognize both risk and opportunity. Sometimes it is as simple as saying yes. I call making luck "connecting the dots." It means approaching the world as if all things were possible—looking at potential connections between things familiar and things unfamiliar. It is more than being open to ideas. It is about smashing ideas together in new ways. It is about being interested in everything and being open to seeing opportunity everywhere.

But just seeing it is not enough. You have to wrestle it to the ground like it's a wild-eyed longhorn steer.

Another tamale story: In San Antonio, the Perez family has been making their own luck since 1952 at Ruben's Drugstore, where they serve the best homemade, slow-cooked pork shoulder tamales you've ever tasted. The Christmas push requires fifteen to eighteen cooks a day working from late November until New Year's Eve. The doors open at 7 a.m., and when it gets close to Christmas the waiting line stretches around two city blocks. The tamales sell for nine dollars a dozen, and you can buy as many as you want. Many customers come from out of town with big ice chests to pack the warm tamales in for the ride home. In one hour on December 23, 2015, they sold a thousand dozen. "People think of our tamales as Christmas," Anita Perez said.[14]

They shut down on New Year's Day and take a well-deserved two-week break. Then they are back at work making luck or tamales or something in between.

Lessons Learned: Cowgirls Design Their Own Lives

- Build your own life timeline. Write it down now! Pay attention to what is important at this very moment, but then think about the rest of your life. Your timeline will be laced with reality and what is known. Look for the inflection points that can open massive opportunity. Then create what I call a "treasure map." This is where dreams and hopes come into play. Layer this into your life timeline. Share it with the important people in your life. Seek their guidance and support.

- Revisit this exercise over and over again. Or, as the phrase goes, "lather, rinse, repeat!"

- I love my family and believe I have done right by them. But I love my career as well. The perfect life balance does not exist, and would probably not be healthy if it did. I wanted both and it was never perfect, but I would not trade anything for it. I look at our children today with an incredible sense of pride.

Mabel Strickland portrait
(Accession Number 2005.232.1 © Dickinson Research Center, National Cowboy & Western Heritage Museum, Oklahoma City, Oklahoma)

Chapter 8

COWGIRLS BUILD A KICK-ASS CULTURE

Mabel Strickland's father introduced her to horses when she was three. She took to them immediately and had a lifelong love affair with them. She started training with a trick rider at an early age and in 1913, at her first rodeo, won the trick riding competition. Talk about a shot of confidence! She was soon invited to join Drumhellers Wild West Productions to hit the road with her trick riding stunts. Word is that she was quite beautiful so her parents said she had to have a chaperone, and then off she went.[15]

She was always lovely and dressed to the nines, so she attracted the attention of rodeo champion Hugh Strickland, and the two were married in 1918. (I guess this is why my mother didn't want me to run off as a barrel racer. I would have probably ended up with a rodeo guy. Funny...I ended up with an old cowboy anyway. He just disguised himself as an ad man for a number of years.)

Mabel is a beacon for us all because not only was she highly honored and awarded in her own right, but she created a culture and atmosphere for others to succeed. However, she did advise her daughter not to follow in her footsteps, because she realized that at some point there might not be any contests left for women to compete in.

She was right. By the Depression years of the 1930s, rodeo opportunities for women had all but disappeared, until 1948 when the Women's Professional Rodeo Association was organized. However, this was just competition among women, unlike in Mabel's day where she competed with men and women.[16]

Mabel Strickland will forever be remembered as the First Lady of Rodeo.

Cowgirls have an amazingly strong sense of culture. They understand the powerful forces that bind people together and tear them apart. Tradition, heritage, faith, a common purpose, pride in work, and love bind us all together. But it is more than just embracing a culture, it is lifting it up like a precious jewel and then making it truly better than just one person could imagine. It builds upon common truths. A kick-ass culture sets you apart from the rest and others cannot help but notice the sparkle.

A CULTURE THAT IS AN UNFAIR COMPETITIVE ADVANTAGE

Building an entire company around the family clan team concept is a big idea that not only works, it creates a powerful advantage for businesses who are bold enough to do so. At T3, we firmly believe our culture sets us apart. We laugh and call it our terribly unfair competitive advantage.

A company's culture is a mystical thing, especially in a creative-driven business like mine. Culture is a moving, breathing organism that is in constant motion and can change on a dime. The good parts must be supported and embraced on a daily basis. Ours is quirky, funny, highly collaborative, tough when we need to be, and has a low tolerance for jerks among many other things. Our teams are smart, fast, strategic, and creative. It is so fun to walk into a meeting where people are laughing, being silly, holding babies on their hips. They don't take themselves too seriously. But they produce awesome results-oriented work and knock the ball out of the park every day. We know our culture is different because clients, employees, analysts, and our partners give us real-time, real-world feedback. We ask them to contrast and compare.

Today, you walk into T3's Austin office and you know you are in a unique, special environment. Our lobby is actually our café. There is a huge video screen that welcomes clients, celebrates new work, and displays profiles of our staff. Big model airplanes hang from the ceiling. There is a basketball scoreboard on the back wall. One big long window ledge is covered with large fossils from West Texas. You'll see an impressive variety of dogs running around, and you'll probably see people carrying babies. People work on big, open floors—everyone visible to everyone. It simply has a wonderful vibe.

In our culture, people visit with each other all the time. There is never a concern that someone might be wasting time by just chatting or harmless gossiping. They are sharing ideas, learning about each other's families, telling funny stories, or sharing interesting insights they have just learned. They build bonds, trust, respect, and friendships all day, every day.

Who owns the culture? The truth is we all do. You know you have been successful when you see your staff take ownership of the culture. They defend it. They tweak it. They do not have to ask permission because it has become theirs just as much as it is mine. And that is just the point. The moments I see that happening are some of the most rewarding experiences I have ever had.

Our T3 & Under program has become our cultural icon. Almost everything we do originates from the bonds formed by this program. For years, we have celebrated our employees, clients, and partners who have new babies by sending them a little pair of bright red leather baby boots, along with a poem about starting your journey as a little cowboy or cowgirl. Those boots usually stay on the dresser in the baby's room until they are old enough to wear them.

We have a disciplined, thoughtful approach to hiring. We go through all of the normal due diligence and first round of interviews that focus on skills and experience, but then we almost always include team members that the candidate will be working with or managing. This is a critical cultural fit filter that gets it right most of the time.

We make a point of recognizing individual effort so that people do not disappear into their teams. Every monthly staff meeting recognizes individual team members who are having an anniversary. And every month we present one team member with the "White Hat" award, which is a big white felt Texas cowboy hat, in recognition for performance that goes above and beyond.

Round-Up is our senior leadership team that focuses on strategic planning issues on a two-year horizon. They meet once a month, review our financial performance, current clients and new business opportunities, and address any other issues. This team is our North Star and operates as a highly effective team. Everyone talks. Questions and new ideas are welcome. Each member has earned respect and genuine regard from everyone else. Some have been with T3 for twenty-five years; some are relative newcomers.

OUR EVENTS DEFINE US

We recently received a call from a potential client who we had been talking to for a long time. He said, "I want to bring my management team up to meet you. Let's do it this Thursday or next Thursday, because I want to be there for the Cool Shit Thursday presentation." Now that is a great phone call. Cool Shit Thursday is a weekly T3 celebration that he had read about on our website. Each Thursday someone volunteers to show off a new technology or a new capability. It has to be inspiring and it has to be fun. Then, if we have a new employee or two, we ask them to be the bartender and serve their favorite cocktail to the entire staff. It is an amazing icebreaker, because they get a fun introduction to everyone.

By the way, the guy who called is now a client! A few of our regular events:

- Breakfast taco Friday mornings, an Austin tradition with an ongoing competition around which restaurant makes the best tacos
- Candy Fridays at 10 a.m. sharp
- Whiskey Friday afternoons, which is an unauthorized tasting of flights of whiskey and a ritual that I have only heard about
- Halloween parties for the kids
- Thanksgiving potluck with way too much food
- Food truck staff lunches in front of our building. The staff

eats lunch on the front steps and waves at all the cars
driving by
- Holiday Cookie Exchange
- Our annual Winter party, which we always have in late
  January after everyone has recovered from the holidays

Our Internal Development department has concierge ser-
vices that will wrap Christmas presents for staff and see that
their dry cleaning and laundry are picked up and delivered.

At the end of our fiscal year, which is September 30, we
do something we call Creative Ranch. We fly all of our staff
from the other offices to Austin and we have three days of
lectures, seminars, and team meetings that are so inspiring.
We always do a five-minute video that shows the body of
work we did during the year. It is a major undertaking. And
the most awesome thing is that it is not in anyone's job
description. It is totally voluntary. We end with an all-staff
celebration marking the end of another successful year in
business and look to the upcoming year with a combination
of hope and energy.

We have a huge rivalry with the other advertising agencies
in Austin over Ping-Pong. There is a big event each year, and
our team is always in the top two or three. We have been
known to fly in a Ping-Pong ringer from our New York office
from time to time, but don't tell anyone.

When the weather permits, my favorite thing to do for the
staff and our clients is to host them at our ranch in the Texas
Hill Country. Families come out and the kids swim in the pool,
take hayrides, ride horses, pet the goats, shoot skeet (highly
supervised), and hang out with our three dogs. Many of our
visitors have never been on a ranch, never shot a gun. Sometimes a small group will spend the night and see the Milky

Way for the first time. Many have never told tall tales while drinking a glass of wine by the campfire.

WE ARE BUILT TO KEEP

Our culture comes from a different business strategy. We built our company because we loved the work and the people, and it has been financially rewarding to our family. But we built it to keep as a long-term family asset. So many of our competitors have built their businesses with a single purpose—to sell them. That creates a huge cultural divide that everyone feels in their hearts. Many of our competitors are now owned by global holding companies where decisions are often made halfway around the world by people the staff has never met and never will. Employees know that while they may respect their managers and love their teammates, they are subject to arbitrary decisions from on high. Now we are seeing agencies that have been acquired multiple times, and that just hollows out a culture. That is not just my opinion, because I know it to be true from talking with our employees. Our company has become a refuge for many talented people who saw their companies' cultures sold out from under them. I cannot tell you how many people have told me that they were simply fed up with the shit show of corporate mergers and acquisitions.

Our teams know that at the end of the day I make the decisions at T3, and they are welcome to come pull up a chair and talk to me about any of them. Our independence has made us a talent magnet. We were doing some planning recently, and one very senior guy who had recently joined T3 after experiencing multiple takeovers at his former employer was asked how he felt about being at T3. His response was "I'm thankful."

Think about how you can pull people together with your own unique culture. It does not have to be expensive or time-consuming. But it does have to have heart and humanity and cowgirl spirit.

COWGIRLS EMBRACE AMBIGUITY

When you own your own company or you are in a major role in a big corporate culture, there is no one telling you what to do. That is why it is so important to be "all in." You have to be in tune with the big issues because it is up to you to sort through them and set the course.

Sometimes there is not a clear direction or answer. A customer needs to do something, but is not sure how to frame the ask. A team member is not clicking well on a project and needs to try a new direction, but is not sure what to do. Many people struggle with these situations. They can be very skillful in planning what to do once a direction is clearly defined. But choosing a direction goes to the core of strategy.

As a leader, embrace ambiguity. This is a powerful tool. Learn to climb the trees and see the forest and the mountains and the ocean. And then, climb back down and lead your team in the right direction.

I have had more than one college professor tell me that during school years and even college, there are assignments—tangible, defined projects—for which specific feedback and grades are given. Students have a more prescriptive environment and they get feedback quickly. When you get out in the business world, sometimes feedback is few and far between, assignments can be ambiguous, and the guardrails fall off.

USE A LOT OF STRAW DOGS

At T3, our approach to ambiguity is to put up what we call a "straw dog." What that means is that it is a safe way to float an idea, because if it gets shot down, it is only straw. You learn to start to work through ambiguity by standing up straw dogs, which incite debate and ideation. When you have something to react to, whether it is right or wrong, you can begin to move the needle. You find things to build upon and things to discard. But no blood is let.

Often our best work comes out of ambiguity because it is not a prescriptive ask. Our clients are asking us for the best way to solve a problem or exploit an opportunity without any preconceived ideas about what that solution might be. General George Patton said, "Never tell people how to do things. Tell them what to do and they will surprise you with their ingenuity."

We teach everyone about straw dogs. They help people sort through ambiguity. A blank wall can be very intimidating and scary for people who are not used to facing one. The world is full of ambiguity. Learn to manage it, shape it, and use it to build your personal power. Go find a colleague and talk it out until the right path is clear. My dad always said, "Sometimes you feel like a frog in a hailstorm. Keep your eyes wide open and pretty soon you will see some light."

BE ABSOLUTELY HONEST WITH YOUR BOSS

A cowgirl always remains responsible for herself. She instinctively puts herself in good situations and navigates away from bad ones. She approaches her first job exactly that way. She is all in. She is candid about what she wants to accomplish. She is assertive and positive. If she has goals, she shares them with her boss. If she has things she really wants to learn, she says so and volunteers to work some extra time to improve her skills. When she is ready for more responsibility, she proudly raises her hand. If something needs to be done, she does it without being asked. She focuses on building rock-solid skills and competence.

Take a real interest in your manager. Learn her leadership style and look for strengths and weaknesses. Find ways to support her and inspire her. Tell her about what makes you tick. Be complementary, a contributor. Always present a problem with a thought-through solution. Share an article that is interesting with your boss and your team. Show a real interest in what is going on. If new positions open up in the company, ask whether you might be qualified for one of them. Or why not? Be positive, upbeat, and consistent about what you want to accomplish in your role.

In return for an all-in approach to your job, proactively discuss with your boss what the guidelines are about work schedule flexibility. Focus the conversation on the quality of your work. Ask for flexibility to go to a school play or get your hair cut without asking for permission. If you commit to not letting any balls drop, why should she care when you leave for lunch? Do this successfully, and you will remove a lot of guilt women feel when they need to deal with family or personal issues. But for it to work, you have to be all in. When you can do more, ask for more. When you don't have other responsibilities, be the first one to arrive and the last one to leave. If you are having a slow day, ask if you can help someone or volunteer to research something.

If your boss is not a good manager, the cowgirl tries to help her improve. Politely. Very few people are really candid and transparent with their boss, and that creates massive barriers. Cowgirls are clear, straightforward, and stand their ground.

Have conversations about promotions and your compensation. But do your homework first. Ask the tough questions about pay equality and benefits. Your biggest leverage is the combination of your personal power and your knowledge about the position. I remember what a Dell client told me years ago: "No one is more interested in your career than you." You have to take ownership of your life and actively manage it.

A CULTURE OF FEARLESSNESS

More than one college professor has told me that her students do not understand how good they are. They do not have the confidence they deserve. The only way for them to understand how good they really are is to dive into their careers and learn from experience.

Build a culture of fearlessness. Create a safe but stimulating environment for people to dive in and learn how competent they really are. A fearless culture encourages everyone to stretch and confront their individual fears and learn to deal with them. Many people don't have clear awareness of their own fears and what triggers them, so they hold back without understanding why. In a fearless culture, people are encouraged to confront those fears and talk about them.

When those fears are laid bare and people come to understand that everyone has their back and will fight to not allow them to fail, you see confidence and assertiveness soar. If you put your heart into something and fall flat on your face, you win respect for trying. That respect brings coaching and a helping hand that moves individuals forward. But, more importantly, it teaches the cultural value of pursuit of excellence. That is where the power is. It is just like the relationship between a cowgirl and her horse: It gets better and stronger over time.

A fearless culture diminishes competitiveness among individuals because the core of the cultural values is cooperation. I was recently in an all-day creative meeting at T3 working on a branding strategy for a client. The team had made some real progress and things were going well. The team leader came back after a break and challenged the entire group to think about things that would cause the project to fail. For the next forty-five minutes, everyone confronted their fears, looked for weaknesses in the plan, and did worst-case scenarios. They looked fear square in the face and left the meeting feeling confident and unafraid. They had looked for the unspoken elephant in the room, confronted it, and turned it into a little armadillo.

In college, I learned something so valuable from Earl Campbell, who ended up being a Heisman Trophy winner and one of the most celebrated football players in the history of Texas football. Sports reporters always asked him, how was he able to perform so well? How could he score so many touchdowns? He never took credit for himself, even though he was physically strong, talented, and a master at self-deprecating humor. He would always answer, "It wasn't me—it was my teammates." And he meant it. He earned the admiration of everyone on the team and everyone in Texas. When Earl succeeded and you were on the team that allowed him to succeed, all of the boats would rise. One of the most uplifting evenings of my university career was the night he won the Heisman. Thousands of students poured into the streets celebrating our admiration for Earl. It still brings a tear to my eye.

Once, early in his career, he was badly injured and sidelined. His football career was in jeopardy. I saw him at an event, shot some informal black-and-white photos of him, and took them to a class that we were in together. I asked him to autograph the photos and he said, "Why do you want my autograph?" I just said, "Because you are going to be famous someday." Boy, did I call that right. I guess it was just my gut feeling shining through. Earl is a winner. He knew how to motivate his team. He was an honorary cowgirl. I am proud to know him.

MEETINGS: THE GOOD. BAD. AND UGLY.

I have been to many uplifting, inspirational meetings. You can almost touch the positive energy and empathy among the participants. There is a camaraderie that signals healthy relationships.

I have also attended bad meetings that suck the life out of you and make you want to run out the door screaming. Look out for any meeting where one person dominates the conversation and few questions are asked and few are answered. I attended a meeting like that last year and afterward told the team leader privately that was the worst meeting I ever attended. A few weeks later it happened again. We now have a new team leader.

I read a *New York Times* article about how men interrupt women in business meetings, and as result, many women simply give up and do not speak at all. Obviously, this gets in the way of effective collaboration. I was taken aback to say the least. Where I come from, if anyone interrupts a cowgirl, they better duck as they do it! No self-respecting cowgirl would put up with such behavior. We have cultural norms "out here" (back at the ranch) that people understand and respect, that come from lessons learned by generations of ranchers. This is simply boorish behavior that any respectable cowgirl would call out.

More than half of the challenges that women face at work are a result of a lack of guiding principles in their workplace. We had two women from T3 attend the 3% Conference recently in New York. The 3% group is focused on getting more women in creative management roles in advertising agencies. They came back with a new respect for our culture and were horrified at the stories they heard about how women are treated in many agencies. Organizations that behave like that, that tolerate behaviors like that, have a flawed culture that comes from weak leadership. Think of the squandered talent. Think of the loss of shareholder value. If they worked for me, they would be kicked out the door with a boot firmly planted on their butts.

Allow me a personal rant on meeting behavior. A few years ago, we were approved to be on the agency roster of a major pharmaceutical company. We had picked up a few successful assignments and were hoping to really grow the business. Another opportunity came our way, so we brought one of our expert teams to New York from Austin to pitch the business.

We had rehearsed, prepared, and had novel ideas to discuss with the clients. Before the meeting, we were really excited and feeling good about our odds to win. After we set up our presentation in the room and everyone was seated, the key client arrived. No sooner had we completed our introductions and exchanged pleasantries than the client buried her face in her iPhone. She texted, giggled, e-mailed, and probably searched for a dinner reservation. It was beyond rude.

Our professionals at T3 continued to present and did a damn great job. The client glanced at our presentation only a couple of times. I wanted to stop and challenge her behavior, but I did not want to embarrass her in front of her team. We left perplexed and ultimately did not get the business. Although I was mad we had wasted our precious time, I knew that we would never be happy working for a client who showed such disrespect.

Lesson learned. Never, ever do that in a meeting, unless you announce to the group ahead of time that your wife is having a baby, and you will be checking messages in case you need to dash off to the hospital. Or you just got a call from your child's school and he is throwing up in the bathroom.

SHOOT THE ASSHOLE AS SOON AS YOU SEE ONE

I was speaking at a conference years ago, and during the question-and-answer period a woman stood up and asked, "How do you maintain your cool culture? How do you make it real for your staff?" I did not hesitate. I looked directly at her and said, "We shoot the assholes."

The crowd roared. That idea became the hit of the entire convention. As I walked through the exhibit hall over the next few days, people would wave and make a little gun with their fingers. I was a cowgirl that day!

Fortunately, I can count on one hand the assholes that we let slip into our company. We weed most of them out in the interview process. But when one gets in, our staff is quick to let me know. Dealing decisively with these people helps avoid complacency in the organization and strengthens our culture because the teams see us aggressively defending it.

I had one very talented guy who was a gifted creative, very insightful, and often ahead of his time. But he had this way of taking personal credit for things that his team accomplished without acknowledging their contributions. It worked OK for a while, but then people started to pull away from him. I had to tell him that he had lost the trust of everyone in the organization. I told him I could not make people want to work for him, only he could do that. He left that day, and happily has done well. Maybe he learned a life lesson that day. Remember, your problem asshole may be a saint to someone else.

I had one recently that I let stay too long. He had this persona that simply created a dark cloud over our collective spirit. Within a few days of his departure, people were talking about how much more fun the café had become without him always watching and judging them. I have learned my lesson: Never, never tolerate an asshole. Fire away the first time you even think someone may have these tendencies. You will rarely be wrong. People will love and admire you forever if you take one out.

I once had a client throw a pen at me across the room because I challenged her thinking in front of her team and her boss. She just lost it. Everyone in the room was appalled. She was a genuine textbook asshole. I got up and left because I thought we were all in danger. Everyone else followed me out the door, including her boss.

Point of clarity: You can have passive-aggressive behavior without having assholes. You rarely have an asshole who does not exhibit passive-aggressive behavior. Assholes only seek power for themselves. Shoot 'em like a snake without any mercy.

Lessons Learned: Cowgirls Build a Kick-Ass Culture

- A company's or family's culture is built step by step, year by year. It becomes what you stand for. Protecting it and building it through trust, creativity, and tradition is the most important thing that great leaders do. Your life will be measured by how passionately you defend it.

- Nothing inspires me today more than a fearless team. Fearless teams are built on trust and know they have each other's backs. I watch these teams every day at T3. They take on any problem with the conviction that they will not only solve it, but it will be a home run. Strive to build and inspire your own fearless teams. And then sit back and watch the exciting results.

Sonora Carver and her diving horse
(Glenbow Archives NB-16-417)

Chapter 9

COWGIRLS KNOW A GOOD IDEA WHEN THEY SEE ONE

When William "Doc" Carver was crossing the Platte River in 1881, there was a bridge collapse and his horse took a dive into the water. That experience led to a crazy big idea—girls on diving horses.

Years later Doc's son, Al Floyd Carver, built the first ramp and tower for diving horses. Then all they needed was the girl.

Ad: "Wanted: Attractive young woman who can swim and dive. Likes horses, desires to travel. See Dr. W.F. Carver, Savannah Hotel." Sonora Webster answered the ad in 1923 and earned a place in circus history. She loved the idea of a diving act, and she wanted to be the one who dazzled the audiences.

To achieve the stunt, the horse was run up the ramp and as it reached the top, Sonora, wearing a red bathing suit, jumped on its back and dove into the water. She was a big hit and soon became the lead act and a huge cash cow. She married Doc's son Floyd in 1928. In 1931 Sonora's horse, Red Lips, dove straight into the water but hit the water off balance. Sonora's eyes were open when she hit the water and she was blinded by retinal detachment. She was blind eleven of the nineteen years of her career and kept it a secret until 1942. She died in 2003 at ninety-nine.

Cowgirls know that you can teach an old dog a new trick. They are always improvising and working on new ideas, ways to enhance their performance, ways to stand out. Cowgirls are creative, fun, full of life, and always trying to move everyone forward. Cowgirls are unafraid of being the center of attention, out in front. They relish applause.

OUR BUSINESS IS ABOUT MANUFACTURING IDEAS

Our business at T3 is to make ideas. Every idea has to be new, unique, and powerful. We make them, release them into the world, and then do it over and over again, year after year. I used to worry that someday the creative juices might slow down or grind to a halt. But the fascinating thing I have seen develop over the last few years is that our creative prowess has actually accelerated, largely because of teamwork. As those teams have developed, matured, and become so empowered, we have seen the quality of our ideas improve again and again.

Ask for ideas. Trade them around. Teach your people that ideas are like dreams. When you are making ideas, put reality aside. Don't worry about reality because it will present itself soon enough. Cowgirls like to lie on their backs in a field of green grass and let ideas float around like clouds in the sky and morph in the summer breeze.

Ideas don't give a damn about gender. But a smart, attractive, confident woman with a big smile on her face because she knows her team "knocked it out of the park" with a big idea is simply irresistible.

GREAT THINGS START WITH A FEW SMALL THINGS

An idea can be a very simple thing. It usually comes from an insight. Years ago we had an opportunity to do a small project for UPS. They were trying to reach out to more diverse suppliers and were looking for better ways to connect (which is why we were talking to them). They were scheduled to attend a supplier diversity convention in a few months and asked us for ideas on how to make their booth more effective in attracting people. It was both a small budget and a huge opportunity.

Our conceptual teams worked on all kinds of ideas and finally settled on one. As you know, conventions involve lots of walking on concrete floors. And women, as crazy as they are (me included), often forgo comfort for more stylish shoes. We capitalized on this simple insight and built an entire campaign about the idea that by the middle of the day most of the women at the convention wished they had gone for comfort instead of style. When women passed by the UPS booth, we offered them a pair of comfy brown slippers with the UPS logo embroidered in pink on each shoe—all each woman had to do was share her e-mail address and sign up for an account, which she gladly did. (Note: It practically took an act of Congress to get UPS to let us use pink logos instead of the standard UPS gold color, but we prevailed.)

Before we knew it, about a third of the women at the conference were wearing the UPS slippers. One panel discussion started with a presenter proudly wearing her UPS slippers on the stage. She threw style out the window and felt empowered by how bold she was. During the panel discussion, the other panelists asked for slippers to be brought up for them. Home run! We knew we had a winner. Several weeks later we saw the results of the e-mail campaign, and it was amazing. A couple of cowgirls on our team had the audacity to see a big idea in a simple insight. Today, UPS is one of our largest, most valued clients, and it all started with a pair of fuzzy, comfy brown house slippers.

Think about your business, your teams. Do they know the folklore of pivotal points in your business? Do they understand how small things turned into big things? These stories provide invaluable lessons and empower teams to follow successful themes. Do you have a way to tell these stories to new employees? Do you have a campfire where you sit around at night and spin these tales? If not, you should.

THE CARE AND FEEDING OF IDEAS

When we are in free-form idea generation mode at T3, we have a cardinal rule—there are no bad ideas. Ideas are respected, documented, and put safely away. We never shoot down an idea when it first appears. Do that and you quickly slow the flow. Ideas want to go to happy places. They do not want to be judged, because even a bad idea can easily spark a great idea.

Years ago H-E-B, a major grocery store chain in Texas, was opening a unique store in Austin called Central Market. It was a concept that took a grocery store to an entirely different level. It was a store for people who were obsessed with food—we know them today as foodies. We were doing some advertising work for H-E-B, and they called us in a panic. The store was scheduled to open in three weeks but they were way behind their hiring goals. The problem was that they were not just looking for employees, they were looking for "foodies"

who were food experts. They had run all of the typical re-
cruitment ads and nothing was working. We assembled a team
and started brainstorming. After about an hour someone said,
"Let's put people on street corners with a sign that says, 'We
Work for Food.'" Everyone laughed and the meeting continued. But we all kept coming back to that quirky idea. We
pitched it to the client and they bravely said yes.

Within a day we had enlisted some Central Market employees and hired a cast of characters. We hand made
signs, printed employment applications, and bought crates
of oranges. We deployed them before dawn on all of the
major street corners in Austin. As the morning traffic
stacked up, our people would wave their signs, hand out
applications, and give everyone an orange. It was on all
the television channel news programs at 6 and 10 p.m. It
was on the front page of the *Austin American-Statesman* the
next morning, and Central Market was flooded with applications. The store opened with a vibrant "foodie" culture
that delivered on the promise. Central Market made a big
contribution to the local food bank that helped homeless
people often seen on those same corners, and continues to
do so to this day.

Don't discard crazy ideas. Put them up on the wall and
watch them for a while.

At T3, we want the team, not individuals, to always own
ideas. Everyone is encouraged to freely build on top of each
other's ideas in something we call iterative development. The
team has to feel that ideas are a collective work product. That
collective ownership gets ego off the table. Collective ownership is why we have seen superstars disappear. Collective
ownership means that there are no good and bad ideas. Some
ideas are more appropriate for a specific situation, but we

cherish and honor all of them, because we have all seen what seemed like a terrible idea morph into something wonderful with just one or two little tweaks.

Cowgirls know that being part of an idea-generating team takes equal parts of bravery (to put your idea out there) and open-mindedness (to listen to and build on other ideas). Our best leaders are orchestrators. They encourage discussion. They create a comfortable place for introverts and younger members to talk. Many times, they are first to throw out silly or incredibly personal ideas to encourage others to share openly without fear.

One of my clients hired us four different times as he rose through the ranks of four pharmaceutical research companies. He was smart and bold. He wanted his brands to stand out in categories that tended to skew to the staid. He could be rough on our creative teams during his first review of our ideas and would almost always send us back to the drawing board. The creative department called him Hurricane Glenn because he would leave our initial thinking in ruins. But they called him that out of respect. He challenged their thinking and brought out their best. One of our writers (who had worked with him in the past) suggested that we simply give him preliminary thinking in the first round, knowing too well that it would never see the light of day. But we never did that. We loved the intellectual sparring, the give-and-take, and the twinkle in his eye when he laid waste to our first campaigns. We always came back stronger in our next round. When he finally said, "that's the one" we knew that he would give our work his full support.

We did one of the boldest campaigns of my career for one of his companies. The campaign focused on how critical relationships and trust played in the decision-making process of his buyers when choosing a pharmaceutical research partner. We used *National Geographic*–style photography to show people from many different cultures who had earned their community's trust. We actually recruited people on the streets of New York to find the interesting characters to photograph.

When his CEO asked to see the print campaign before it was shipped off to publications, our client was afraid that the CEO might kill it because it was so bold. He hid the artwork in his red Corvette and sped out of the office parking lot, not to be seen again for several days. The CEO saw the campaign for the first time when the ads were published in the trade magazines, when it was much too late to object. It was more than disruptive in the industry, and my client became both famous and infamous as a marketer who knew no fear. He is a dear friend to this day.

Think about your organization and how it treats ideas. Being a champion for ideas, and championing healthy, passionate, high-functioning teams with passion for what they do is a powerful role for cowgirls to take on.

COWGIRLS NUDGE PEOPLE INTO THEIR BEST ROLES

Ideas provide an amazing pathway to power. Cowgirls respect how different people contribute to an idea's success in radically different ways because they understand that ideas need support to come to life. This sixth sense, this intuition, is the "secret sauce" that holds teams together.

These contributions can be radically different from each other. Cowgirls know that some people are great at developing amazing new ideas. For others, their power comes from nurturing ideas out of other people and then fiercely protecting them from being shot down too. Others contribute by smashing two seemingly unrelated ideas together into something entirely new. Some find their power by waiting until all the ideas are collected and then leading the team through a thoughtful evaluation process to pick the very best one. Some excel at going out and selling the idea. And others contribute by sending out the bill for the idea and collecting the money. Very different talents, but all critical to producing the best work.

I was talking to our youngest son, Sam, about women's intuition the other day. He totally agreed with me and told me a story about running a marketing meeting and having a woman on the team slip him a note that someone in the meeting was crying. Sam said, "I had no idea." They stopped, addressed the issue, and moved on, but without the female staffer pointing out the problem, Sam would not have even noticed. Sam has many talents, but being a big "feeler" is not one of them.

WALK AWAY WHEN YOU CAN

"Leave it" is a traditional command for herding dogs. I never understood this terminology until we started hanging out with Henry and our Border Collies. For them, this command means that the job is over. They can be frantically herding sheep or goats and if you say "Leave it," they will calmly turn and walk away from the excitement of herding. For me, it means, walk away, take a break, and give yourself time to get a fresh perspective. Border Collies teach us a lot about being focused, but stopping the pursuit for a bit to regroup is an important skill as well.

When time permits, we like to generate ideas and maybe group them into big buckets and then walk away from them for at least a day. This step tempers the excitement and gives both the head and the gut a chance to mull things over.

IDEAS WITHOUT EXECUTION ARE JUST WORDS ON A PAGE

We cherish good ideas because of their potential power, but without the ability to execute them, they languish as just ideas. Only when an idea is well executed does it become powerful, even brilliant. Ideas are lofty things. They know no bounds. They float around on the wind currents like dreams. Until they are sold.

Suddenly those big white fluffy ideas have budgets, deadlines, technical specifications, strategic implications, legal implications and compliance issues, and have to work flawlessly on millions of big and little screens. In our business, this is where dreams intersect with reality. And cowgirls are often the ones that pull it all together and make it work.

At T3, our first responsibility is to do no harm to the idea. If you do not fiercely protect it, it will get pushed and shoved around and, when it is finally complete, you won't even recognize it. Ideas must be protected at every step along the way.

We have always excelled at execution. Our company is built to support big companies that need high-end marketing solutions. We are built for big, ongoing programs. We have developed systems, processes, checklists, technical expertise, and infrastructure to do work on a massive scale. When a project moves into execution mode, we run it very much like a software company does with bug tracking software: agile development methods and project management teams that watch it every step of the way. It is one very well-oiled machine, and it is awesome to see it work every single day. Our clients consistently tell us how well we do at getting the work done. We literally release new work every day.

As we do the work we hold ourselves to two standards. First, is it as innovative as it can be? Have we pushed the envelope? Have we looked for unexpected connections? Second, does it have humanity? Does the work speak to people emotionally, does it inspire people, make them laugh, or challenge their thinking?

Every person at T3 understands both of these standards. If during the execution process anyone feels we are missing either one, they are obligated to raise their hand and express their concerns. The cardinal sin at T3 is if you do *not* raise the red flag the moment you see something going awry. We can fix almost anything if we catch it early on.

When a big job is finally launched, we celebrate—with our clients, with our staff, and with our partners. We have a Slack channel called "#proudofthis" where all new work is immediately shared with everyone in the company. People are recognized and thanked. And each time a job is launched, our people raise the bar and create higher expectations for themselves.

Be sure to celebrate the good work you do. Recognize the skill, hard work, and team effort when something good happens. Cowgirls know that a thank-you goes a long way. And when things don't go well, cowgirls look it square in the eye. If we lose, how can we learn from it and win the next time?

HAVE FUN WITH CREATIVE IDEAS

One time I was talking to a really smart CEO who had a successful tech start-up. We talked about business for a while, but then he asked me a rather interesting question. Apparently, he had admired a strong, beautiful, successful woman from afar for quite some time. Turns out they had a mutual friend, so he had attempted to use the name of that friend and sent the woman an e-mail as an introduction. It was a plain and simple e-mail about how he would like to invite her to have lunch or a drink.

He sent that e-mail and waited, and waited. A few weeks had gone by and he got no response from her. He was stumped but determined, and asked me how in the world he could get her to talk to him.

The next afternoon I drove out to the ranch and posed this question to my husband, Lee. So, as we always do when we get a request, we started brainstorming creative ideas on how this guy could break through. After all, being in the advertising business, that is what we do. Help clients break through the clutter and get results.

In about an hour, we crafted an e-mail for my CEO friend to send the woman he was interested in. Leaving it up to him to put together the final wording, based on his own preferences, the e-mail went something like this:

Hello,

I have been wanting to ask you some burning questions.

1. How many angels can fit on the head of a pin?

2. Have you ever killed a deer?

3. When was the last time you ate at Dan's Hamburgers?

He continued with a list of at least twenty of these questions and then closed with:

It is apparent that we have a lot to talk about. So, please meet me for lunch on [date] at [you pick the place].

He sent it, and guess what? He got a fast response and a date. He was blown away. The whole point of this is that you should try to take a creative approach in everything you do. Go try this on something you think is mundane today!

IT IS OK TO HAVE IDEAS

When I speak about many of these concepts to various groups, a question I frequently get is from people who do not feel like their organization is open to new ideas. My first response is always, "Well, that just sucks!" It usually takes the negative spin off the question and lets me respond with a better answer.

I tell my audience that if you find yourself in one of those situations, be a cowgirl, blaze the trail, and teach idea making. I ask them to think of themselves as members of British naval intelligence in World War II. Members of MI5 were masters at deception. They ran Operation Mincemeat, where they put a corpse ashore on the Spanish coastline with clues planted in pockets that were designed to mislead German intelligence. It was crazy, bold, and completely unorthodox. It worked and, just perhaps, helped win the war.

Brace yourself, because you are going to need that kind of courage and creative energy if you are going to open your company to ideas. Go change the culture, but never tell anyone what you are doing. If you are working in a low-idea culture, your idea about ideas won't be very well received. Go get a small whiteboard and a pile of sticky notes and start putting a few ideas up on the wall. You have baited the trap, now just wait.

Someone will ask you what you are doing. You respond by saying, "I'm just trying to figure out which of these choices is best. What do you think?" Boom! You have set the hook. Go slow. Be patient. If they accuse you of promoting ideas, deny it! Never admit to anything.

PAINTING CAREER DELAYED BY THIRTY-EIGHT YEARS

Remember, success is never a straight line. Here is a story that started when I was two years old and my mom handed me a paintbrush. It played out over the next fifty-eight years. It happened because I built buckets and buckets of goodwill along the way that enabled so many connections to happen. You never know what magic and miracles are in store, if you value your network and do interesting things.

It continues with my relationship with my wonderful high school art teacher Carolyn Hayes. She was a real cowgirl and a great artist, but also an even greater teacher. She helped me push and explore my artistic abilities and introduced students in our small town of Liberty, Texas, to the likes of Van Gogh, Chagall, Monet, Rembrandt, and modern artists like Jackson Pollock and Alexander Calder. I was intrigued by their techniques and explored with my paintbrush and drawing pencils.

Carolyn was the reason I decided to major in art in college. My art was featured at local banks and businesses with blue ribbons hanging on my work. A shot of confidence to be sure.

Yes, Carolyn was a cowgirl. Not only did she have a lifelong love affair with horses, but she was always honest in her critique of my work. Never pulled punches. She was my horse trainer, but in art, if I needed to work harder on something or rethink an approach, she gave it to me in straight-shooting language. I took it because I wanted to improve.

In 2006, a couple of years after I joined C200, I had the opportunity to go with some other members of the group on a State Department trip to the Middle East. Five of us met several days before the conference in Egypt just to see the sights. We all became fast friends, but one person in particular, Marcy Maguire, who was also a C200 member, became one of my best friends. Eight years later, that friendship led to an invitation that would change my life.

In 2014, I returned to my roots as an art major and began painting again. I explored a lot of different styles from realistic to abstract. I painted only outside in the elements at our ranch. My work was all over the place, but I felt like it had promise. Lee told me that he was glad I was enjoying painting again, but that I was never going to make one thin dime from my paintings—and that was OK.

That same year, Marcy invited me to a Harvard Business School night at the Curator Gallery in New York, owned by Ann Moore, the former chairman and CEO of Time Inc. I had met Ann Moore years before when she gave a speech, and we became acquaintances through C200. I reconnected with Ann and learned that she had bought the gallery because of her passion for art, and it was going to be act 2 of her career. Remember, it is never too late to reinvent yourself.

Also that night, I met one of Ann's friends and popular curator, Rebecca Michelman. I was bold enough (yet a bit afraid) to ask Rebecca to look at my paintings and showed her a few pictures. She said, "All I can tell you is to keep painting and exploring techniques." Several months later, she volunteered to come to our ranch in Texas, where I was doing all of my painting, and to critique my work.

She and her husband and children came and spent a wonderful weekend with us. Finally, when the kids were happily engaged in the swimming pool, she took a serious look at the work. She quickly began eliminating paintings, being brutally honest with me about what she thought. This went on for a couple of hours and she had eliminated almost everything, but there were two or three paintings left. These were abstract paintings of big dramatic Texas sunsets and sunrises, painted with sweeping horizontal mixes of color. "This is it. Paint like this and we'll do a show in New York," she told me.

I worked my butt off painting for almost a year, always outside (en plein air) at the ranch. Sometimes I bundled up and worked in freezing weather, sometimes it was hotter than nine kinds of hell. But I brushed the sweat off of my face and painted with determination and passion. It was a huge undertaking and I finished over fifty paintings in my "spare time" in the style Rebecca championed. My faithful dogs and loyal companions were always at my side.

So in April 2016, I ended up with a monthlong one-woman show at the Curator Gallery in New York. It has to be one of the most exciting things that ever happened to me! So many friends and colleagues visited during the thirty days of the show, and we sold paintings. Ann Moore told a group who visited the gallery a couple of weeks after the opening, "Those rowdy Texans came and just ravaged the show!" We broke all the gallery sales records.

I was a bit intimidated by the entire process. My curator, and the media for starters. However, one person in particular got my goat. She handled public relations for the gallery. Cool as a cucumber, svelte and attractive, she gave off a knowing air that had me on my guard. I got to know her, and found she is a lovely, caring mother and now a friend. She just knew things about getting PR for an art show that I knew nothing about. She taught me a lot.

No one was more proud of me than my high school art teacher, Carolyn. When I opened the show in NYC, I sent her a text message. She was thrilled and so encouraging. I also asked her what she was working on and she simply said: "A sculpture of my horse." She was one of those people who sometimes magically appear in our lives providing the right influence at the right time.

I continue to have exhibits and sell my paintings. When I got my first check for my art, I called Lee and told him he had to eat crow. I made more than one dime as an artist.

Success is not a straight line.

Lessons Learned: Cowgirls Know a Good Idea When They See One

- Young ideas need to be protected and nurtured. Let them mature before you judge them. Give them time while you watch the changes in circumstances. Like a gangly little foal matures into a magnificent horse, good ideas have a way of rising to the top.
- But a good idea is only that. Great execution is what pumps life into these ideas. Without detailed and relentless

follow-through, ideas will languish and never see the light of day. They will never reach their potential to change lives and situations.

- While you are ideating about yourself and your life, never forget to reinvent yourself. Do it over and over again. It is never too late, and it will make you both happy and interesting. Trust me on this one!

Alice Sisty doing a Roman Stand
(Accession Number 79.026.2901 © Dickinson Research Center,
National Cowboy & Western Heritage Museum, Oklahoma City, Oklahoma)

Chapter 10

COWGIRLS ARE FEARLESS
LEADERS

Alice Sisty was destined for a career as a teacher. After one year of study, she went out west to a dude ranch and fell in love with a horse named Spot-Tail. She didn't want to leave him in Nevada, so a plan evolved where she could keep the horse if she rode him from Reno to New York on a bet. She won the bet.

The ride brought her a great deal of attention, and soon after she decided to be a rodeo rider and forget that teacher's training. This classic photo of Alice performing her "Roman Jump," standing on two horses jumping over a car, just screams fearlessness.

Alice was five-foot-two and barely 105 pounds with her show gear on. Did anything make her tremble in her size 4 boots? Not much. She attempted incredibly dangerous stunts and succeeded over and over. She won high points in such events as bronc, steer, and relay riding, winning all-around champion of cowgirls in Madison Square Garden in 1932, making her a leader of her peers.

After marrying Milt Hinkle, the head of the rodeo, she was asked if she was ready to settle down. This was Alice's reply: "I should say not. I'm happily married, but I'm afraid I wouldn't be if I had to give up my saddle for a kitchen range and a washing machine." I had to laugh at this. The only thing this fearless leader feared was getting stuck with the household chores![17]

Alice Sisty was daring, bold, and a leader.

Cowgirls openly embrace leadership because of the way they have been taught. They view leadership as an opportunity to help people, to move them in the right direction. Cowgirls see leadership as an opportunity and responsibility to pass on the values that they have been given. They understand how to empower and inspire people in ways only a cowgirl can do.

When we think of leadership, we immediately think top down. We think of strong individuals. We think command and control. We think of leadership as always framed in masculine terms. But when you ask both men and women what kind of a leader they would prefer to work for, you get more feminine words. Words like "compassionate," "organized," and "honest."[18] When was the last time you heard a male leader described as compassionate, organized, and honest?

This is a deep vein for cowgirls to mine to find their personal power. This is where you build long-lasting alliances. This is where you build and earn loyalty. This is where you fill your buckets with goodwill.

WHY WE NEED WOMEN LEADERSHIP

My mother-in-law was a protégé of J. Frank Dobie, a famous Texas folklorist in the 1950s and 1960s. Dobie wrote tales of South Texas that he had heard from old cowboys. When asked if the stories were true or not, he would always answer, "Well, if it isn't true, it should be," with a twinkle in his eye.

That statement has stayed with me throughout my career and sums up my view on how women should think about leadership roles. It means we should always reach for our dreams, and just because it is not true today, doesn't mean that with hard work, determination, boldness, and connections you cannot achieve what would seem like the impossible. But in the context of leadership it means more to me; it means that when you step into a leadership role, you take on the responsibility for making dreams come through for everyone in your organization. You take on the responsibility to make things better and, as a woman, you get to define what "better" means. I did not realize it at the time, but that is exactly what I did when I started T3 & Under.

One of the great projects we have worked on with UPS is their "Wishes Delivered" campaign. This is where there is a well-deserving person or organization in need, and UPS surprises them and fulfills their wishes. It has been heartwarming to see schoolteachers get a delivery of needed supplies for their classrooms that were otherwise unfunded. Our role is to make sure all of this is captured on video, and we help them tell the story. Here is the definition exemplified where UPS says, "Well, if it isn't true, it should be." And they make dreams and wishes come true.

From my perspective, shifting into leadership roles is one of the most powerful things you can do. Leadership means enabling people to be the best they can be—to encourage people, challenge them, and kick them in the butt if they slack off. As leaders, women have high standards for achieving results. But they can lead with compassion, building a nurturing and supportive environment that is a better place to be for both men and women. That environment will undoubtedly yield remarkable results.

To me, leadership is the power to do good for everyone. That is why I spend my time encouraging women to step up and lead in the workplace.

COWGIRLS MAKE BETTER LEADERS

Corinne Post, associate professor of management at Lehigh University, decided to see if it could be proven that women make better leaders. She looked at team leadership and women who served on boards. What were the things that make women better leaders? Her hypothesis was a familiar one: that more work in large organizations was being done by teams and that women are more relationship oriented than men. So, would women make better leaders because of their heightened sensitivity to foster collaboration and trust?

She looked at eighty-two teams with more than eight hundred people at twenty-nine leading research and development companies. The study was supported in part by a National Science Foundation grant. Here is what she learned:

- Women excelled in bringing large teams together, especially teams who come from different departments and specialties and who are spread out geographically.
- Women excelled at fostering cross-departmental collaboration, like bridging between technical and creative teams and avoiding turf wars.
- Women were better at letting everyone be heard, even over long distances.[19]

My experience is very much in line with the findings of this study. Women have an innate ability to build high-quality relationships across big, complex groups, often in multiple locations. In my experience, women are more sensitive to other people's nonverbal reactions than most men. Women can see around emotional corners and see things men often miss. They will explore and understand the problem and then set out to fix it, down to the last detail.

I have seen this play out over many years at T3. Our people work on big, complex teams. It is not unusual for there to be fifty people or more working on a project when you add up agency people, clients, and third-party players, and they are usually in many different locations. I have watched our women leaders be the glue that holds these teams together, helps them grow and achieve success over and over again. They are incredibly powerful cowgirls.

FIND CHANGE AND HUG IT LIKE A LONG-LOST LOVE

Some people do not like change. I love it! If I can get my arms around it, I'll give it a big old hug. Why? Because I have learned that with almost all significant change, opportunities emerge if you look for them. Of course, this is not always true, but for me it has been true more often than not. Sometimes when things change I can almost smell opportunity.

Deal with change head-on. Do what needs to be done. But when you can catch your breath, look under the rocks for the underlying opportunities, because they are usually there.

Some change comes at you like a hurricane. I remember in the very early days of the Internet we had a management meeting and were talking about where the business was going. Someone got up and started drawing on a whiteboard. He drew a big circle and labeled it "Internet." He drew lots of other little circles around the big one and connected them

with lines to the big one. The little circles were named TV, radio, magazines, newspapers, direct mail, etc. That scribble on
a whiteboard changed our business forever. Be open to both
incremental change and to tectonic change.

DO THINGS YOU HAVE NEVER DONE BEFORE

Throughout my career I have had clients ask me if I could
do something, and I would answer, almost without exception,
yes. Some of those requests were for things I had done many
times before. But sometimes, it would be for something we
had never done before. This is where the idea of embracing
ambiguity is so powerful. This is where the skies open, the sun
comes out, and you see forever.

There is always a first time. Some people would say, "No, I
cannot do that because I don't have any experience." I spent
all of my career saying yes, often knowing full well that we had
never done it before. How did we pull it off? Because at T3 we
built a culture based on constant learning. We are a learning
organization. We have the skills to learn new solutions fast. It
motivates our people. Many of them are quick studies and can
become experts on something almost overnight, making them
invaluable.

When my husband brought the first Apple computer into
our office, the creative staff threw up their hands and said the
world was about to end. Computers in those days did not kern
type well, and there were those annoying spinning stars and
happy faces hopping around the screen. Later, he brought the
Internet into our business, and again the Luddites screamed
to high heaven that it would be the end of us. Then, when he
installed a video production studio designed for creating low-

cost videos for the Internet, they thought the end of the world was at hand. Actually, each of those changes represented massive opportunity for our company, and the fact that we were an early adopter in each area served us well. I had the ability to calm the masses and hold their hands when Lee wheeled in the change agents.

Speaking of Luddites, I once had a client who ran a rehabilitation hospital in Central Texas. We did all of our work on either telephone calls or personal visits. The CEO absolutely refused to allow a fax machine on the premises. He said it would ruin everything because he would be forced to make decisions too fast, that he needed time to mull things over. One day he asked us to take on a major opening of another hospital, and the work volume and deadlines intensified. We got it done in record time because I snuck a fax machine into his executive assistant's office and did business with her all day, every day. He never knew. Every smart cowgirl knows that there is more than one way to skin a cat. Now some of you say, "What's a fax machine?"!

When opportunity rises up in front of you, grab it and ride right at it. Be open to doing things you have never done before. Do not allow yourself to live in a rut. Develop the skill to figure out new stuff. Do not be constrained by what you know today.

One more tamale story: It was called the "Great Tamale Incident" when President Gerald Ford did something he had never done before. When he visited the Alamo in 1976, he started to bite into a tamale that was still wrapped in its corn husk. San Antonio Mayor Lila Cockrell said, "The president didn't know any better. It was obvious he didn't get a briefing on the eating of tamales."[20] Veteran CBS news reporter Bob Schieffer recalled that the president "nearly choked." Ap-

parently, one of the Daughters of the Republic of Texas got
to the president quickly and removed the corn wrapper before
returning the plate to him. Mike Huckabee said, "Every news-
cast in Texas all weekend long, all they did was show Gerald
Ford not knowing how to eat a tamale. To this day I am convinced that it was that gaffe with the tamale that cost him the
state of Texas. Carter won Texas and Carter won the presi-
dency, and it may have been a tamale that did it."[21]

Lesson learned; if you are going to try something new, get
briefed first, carefully unwrap it, and then take a big bite.

COWGIRLS BUILD POWERFUL NETWORKS

When I was a little girl, I was at a dance with my parents. A
tall, lanky Texan named Buck Echols came over and asked me
to dance. I was surprised and flattered. I stepped on top of his
boots and, as we danced, he told me, "Always remember, Gay,
that your first dance was with a Texas Ranger." And yes, he
was wearing his hat, his badge, and his gun. In those days, no
one was more respected than a Texas Ranger. I remember it
like it was yesterday.

When I went to the University of Texas in Austin, I drove
back and forth to Liberty often. These were the days of CB
radios and my handle was "Sunshine Girl." I was notorious
for having a heavy foot on the gas because I thought my CB
buddies would protect me from the Texas Highway Patrol.
But they didn't. I got a lot of speeding tickets. When I did,
I would call Buck Echols and tell him what county it was in
and the name of the presiding judge and ask his opinion if the
fine was fair. At the time, ticket costs were arbitrarily set by
each judge. I would rant and rave about how unfair it was that

the fines fluctuated so much. Buck would laugh, remind me of our dance, and somehow the charges against me just vanished. That was my first lesson in the power of networks.

When I think about networking, I am reminded of what my mother's teacher told her after she lost her arm to cancer as a young girl, "You can put yourself out there and be all you can be." That, to me, is the perfect definition of networking.

It means that you are willing to make a major investment in becoming a player in your field. That takes time and effort. It means that you get your numbers up, that you are talking to enough people to make your chances of success go up dramatically—to make your own luck. If your market is local, the chamber of commerce might be a good start. If your market is national, then it means attending national conferences, trade shows, and conventions. Focus only on opportunities that can scale, do not waste your time on things that do not have lots of potential to grow if you do a good job.

Be strategic about where you spend your time. I never was very active in advertising organizations because there was no one there who could ever hire me. Instead, I've always gone to conferences where there is a broad cross section of potential clients. I focus on diversity events like Women's Business Enterprise National Council (WBENC) and media events like TED, *Fortune*'s Most Powerful Women, and other thought leadership conferences. I also like smaller events, where you really have an opportunity to get to know people. C200 has lots of these and they are always great. Over the years, I have earned the right to attend these high-powered events. Earlier in my career I started small and worked my way up.

When an opportunity presents itself, act fast. I heard the senior vice president of e-business at Allstate speak at an Allstate Supplier Diversity Exchange about the kind of partners they were looking for. As soon as he finished, I walked up to him and introduced myself. I quickly explained why I thought T3 would be a good fit for Allstate. His team vetted us, asked for a meeting, and they are now one of our largest clients.

Networking is not about asking for favors and advice. It is about building solid relationships with helpfulness and reciprocity. If I can help you, I'll do it without any expectation of getting anything in return. But, if at some time in the future, you find a way to help me, make an introduction or just call up and ask how I'm doing, then we both win and the bonds get stronger.

What do you want to accomplish with your network? The answer to this question will change over time. Early in my career I focused my network on finding job opportunities. Later, the focus changed to finding clients. Then it shifted again to learning from successful, powerful women. And now, it is focused on finding powerful ways to help others.

I have several buckets of networks. Some are business relationships. Some are governmental and political connections. Some are volunteer groups. Others are experts in fields in my own industry, and the surprising thing is how many times they overlap.

COWGIRLS NETWORK TO BE ALL THAT THEY CAN BE

I love the words "be all you can be" because that is the "why" behind networking. "Be all you can be" is a decision you make about how to live your life.

My cowgirls loved to perform in front of huge crowds. Cheers and applause just egged them on to take bigger risks and be more outrageous. They made the choice to play on a big stage, and many of them became the superstars of their day.

The reason to build a network is to help people see who you are, understand what you do, and look for ways to make connections and be helpful. The question becomes, how big is it "to be all you can be"? Is it in a small East Texas town? Is it in a big city? Your state? Nationally? Globally? Each one is a decision. The question becomes, how do you want to distinguish yourself and to whom? There are many ways to do this.

I blog regularly for both *Forbes* and *Fortune* magazines about the entrepreneurial spirit. In the process of writing those posts, I interview all kinds of entrepreneurs. One was a fourteen-year-old boy who was promoting his lawn-mowing business. Another was a fascinating woman who uses horses to teach teams how to better relate to each other. We post many of these articles on LinkedIn. I tweet about business events and use Facebook and Instagram just for fun. I speak nationally and globally. I lecture at quite a few universities. I have built a pretty big platform. It has been a conscious choice because I love being center stage, just like my cowgirls—and, it has been a great way to build my business.

Let me be clear. This is not about bragging and inflating your ego. This is where you build your own brand. This is where you make your mark about who you are. If you don't do it, who will? Think about how big a field you want to play on and go do it. You are in control, and you can make that field bigger or smaller at the right times in your life.

If you want to distinguish yourself, put yourself out there. The bread crumbs you leave along the way can and will appear years later.

Oh. Here is my pet peeve on networking: Do not send me a request to connect on LinkedIn without explaining why you want to connect. I get these stupid requests such as someone in Norway wanting to join my network without any explanation of who they are and why they are interested in me. That is just plain lazy.

BE A RAINMAKER

Sitting around the kitchen table when I was growing up, the conversation was most likely to include whether or not it was going to rain. My father's surveying business ebbed and flowed based on the number of days they could be in the field. My godfather's rice farm and cattle ranch literally could be made or broken by getting rain at the right time of year. Perhaps this understanding of how essential rain was to business made me want to be a rainmaker. If I could make it rain, then everyone would be happy, prosperous, and celebratory. What a great thing to do!

Early on in my career I looked for ways to help grow business in every company I worked for. Sometimes it was easier when the economy was good and business was flowing freely everywhere. But what separates the girls from the cowgirls is being able to make it rain when there is a drought and business is hard to come by.

These are the times you must be resourceful. Not only do you draw on your network but you must also be persistent, not a pest. I have found that most people don't bring in new business because they simply fail to follow up. And I don't mean just sending cookie-cutter e-mails. I mean, real, meaningful follow-up. Do something that will help your potential customer in his or her career. What insights can you offer that no one else has taken the time to think about?

Another fortunate thing I have been able to do through the years is draw on other happy clients to refer us business. This is all about the buckets of goodwill because of honest, hard work I have earned. It means I am willing to do the same for them when they need help. Remember, it is all about reciprocity.

Rainmaking is about literally showing up. In person. At their doorstep. Of course, not a surprise drop-in, but taking the time to go where your potential clients are, and inviting them to review and critique something new and cool you are working on. No pressure, just looking for their opinion. I cannot think of anything I have ever done that has won me more respect and power among my team than to bring home the bacon! Or, of course, to make it rain.

Not long after Lee and I got married, we took a trip to Puerto Rico and attended a seminar for advertising agency people to help them learn how to attract new business. The speaker taught us one important lesson: "If I call your five top prospects and ask them which agency really, really wants their business and they don't name you in the top two or three, you don't even have a new business program."

We decided that insight was valuable enough, so we snuck off and went to the island of Vieques on a mini-honeymoon. When we arrived at the hotel, it looked like something out of *The Night of the Iguana*. Everything was overgrown and there was weird statuary everywhere. We finally met the owner and he asked how many nights we were staying. We said two. He said, "After two nights here, you will come back to me begging on your knees to stay longer." He was right, we stayed a week. He also told us that if we conceived a child while we were there and named the child Irving after him, he would pay for his or her Harvard education!

When we sat down for our dinner, he brought out the wine list. Number 1 was red. Number 2 was white. The list read, "Please order by number."

GET COMFORTABLE WITH RISK

Lee's mother, Isabel, and I hit it off immediately, because she was, among many other things, a real cowgirl. Somehow we just clicked and she became my greatest champion and advocate, as my mom was. In her younger days, Isabel was an expert horse trainer. She could brand, work cattle with the best of them, and field dress a deer without ruining her freshly polished nails.

I was in South Texas one weekend in 1989, the year I started my company. While visiting with Isabel I saw a little blue-and-white-enamel box on her living room table. On the top of the box, in elegant cursive, was this phrase: "Everything is sweetened by risk." I was drawn to that box, and picked it up and held it. It spoke to me—with a comforting message at a time of enormous risk with my new company. Isabel saw me holding the box and, at the end of our visit, she gave it to me.

I still keep Isabel's gift on my desk. Every time I look at it, I am reminded of the lessons that she taught me that day: that without risk there is no gain—that if you never take risks, you will miss out on a lot of the sweetness that life has to offer.

"Everything is sweetened by risk." That has been my experience. When I first started the company, I told people that I ate risk for breakfast every morning. The interesting thing that happens to risk takers is that you learn a lot of lessons that people who don't take risks never learn. Smart risk takers tend to take lots of small risks. Small risks are not going to take you down. But lots and lots of small risks can yield very powerful advancements. You learn how to mitigate risk. You test the waters. You take incremental steps. You learn from failure, but you do not stop advancing. And you gradually get better at it. With each risk you take, your gut learns a lesson. Spend much of a lifetime taking risks, and your instincts will be really, really good.

Risk is a fundamental part of a successful life. You take a risk by accepting a new job, by deciding who you spend time with, by what you do and where you go. Avoiding risk means that you will miss out on life's biggest thrills, lessons, and accomplishments.

Risk tends to come at you quickly. Learn to get the facts, think it through, listen carefully to your gut, and make a decision. Do not overthink it. Do not worry about it. Make the call and move on. Some of the best decisions I have ever made were made on the spot, literally within moments.

Knowing when and where to accept levels of risk is a huge source of personal power. Taking risks sets you up to fail or advance. Not taking risks leaves you with the status quo, at best. Every time you take a risk, you are testing yourself. Be brave and take a chance to jump ahead of the game.

GIVE YOUR POWER AWAY

One of the most effective things you can do as a manager is to give your power away. If you give your people the power to make their own calls, everyone will be stronger. What I have learned is that you have to explicitly grant authority for it to be effective. If you specifically grant power, your people will be much more likely to use it.

In our company, two of our most important jobs are the creative director and the account director. They are powerful positions because they have the authority to decide if a piece of work is good enough to be presented to our clients. The creative director works with the creative teams to develop ideas, to improve on them, to rework them. The account director focuses on whether the idea is the best choice for our client strategically and economically. At the end of the day, they both make the final call about whether it goes out the door.

Giving that power to a person who has earned it is one of the most thrilling, rewarding things I get to do. When I promote someone into one of those two positions, it means I have total faith that the right decisions will be made.

Give your power away. Move people up. Empower them to make their own choices. As I have done this over the years, I have been fired from every job title at T3 I ever had because the people I promoted were better than I was. Hire great, capable people and they will take your job, which for me has been a wonderful thing. Right now I feel pretty safe as CEO and master connector.

TURNING OVER THE BOOKS

Shortly after starting T3 I realized that doing our books wasn't the highest and best use of my time. Because we were crawling out of a deep recession, there happened to be a program sponsored by the government that put willing people who had been laid off for no fault of their own into a training program. The program helped them with interviewing skills, networking, and learning how to transfer their talents into a different industry.

It was through this program that I was introduced to a woman who could potentially help with our accounting needs. She was unassuming, but confident and capable. I hired her and, to my great surprise, half of her salary was covered by the government program for six months. It gave the employer only half the risk of a new hire. We both had skin in the game.

As we got to know each other, I realized that she had grown

up in a small town in Central Texas and shared the same ethics and grit that our company did. Her family had lived around the world when her father was in diplomatic service, but she spent most of her life on her family ranch in Texas. She is as honest as the day is long and stands by her word.

A note about her family: Her mother is one tough, hardworking character. After losing her husband, she never flinched at the ranch duties, including the task of cutting and baling her own hay. At one point she decided to sell her hay-baling equipment, and we sent our ranch foreman, Hardy, to go take a look at it. At the end of the inspection, he offered to buy it and they made a deal. He recalls that her handshake almost broke his hand. Wow—she is a cowgirl with a capital "C"!

Long story short, her daughter, who was shepherding our accounting through rapid growth and changes in the ad industry, was growing into a powerful leader at T3. Again, not the top-down authoritative type, but building her team on accuracy, results, goodwill, and camaraderie. Hers is the longest-tenured team at T3.

Today that young staff accountant is now the CFO of T3. Step by step she earned the right to join the C-suite. She is a cowgirl and the Rock of Gibraltar to me and my family.

WHAT YOU DON'T DO IS MORE IMPORTANT THAN WHAT YOU DO

I heard Ann Moore give a speech, and she used this Nelson Mandela quote, "No is a complete sentence." I learned that valuable lesson early in my career in the advertising business.

Small clients without vision and adequate budgets soon make you feel like you are being nibbled to death by ducks.

We say no to nine out of ten client inquiries we get. We have developed a ten-point new business filter that has been in place for years. We go through the checklist every time a new opportunity presents itself. The first question we ask ourselves is whether we would want to work for the company. A no immediately ends the conversation.

No empowers you. No allows you to laser focus in on what is important. No simplifies your life. In 2000, Austin was full of Internet start-ups rich with venture money. They clamored to our office all claiming to have a $12 million budget and demanding that we get their ads placed in the Super Bowl—even though it had been sold out for months. We had so many of them coming and going that we could not get any real work done. We told all but one of them no. And the one we did take was a mistake. But my CFO and I got tougher than nickel steaks and we collected every dime they owed us. It took months, but we prevailed with persistence.

When life gets complicated, stop and prioritize what the most important things are that you do. Look at the bottom third of the list and see what you can cut and where you can say no. As you build your personal power, raise a family, and succeed in your career, you must draw the lines. It is so easy to get overcommitted. It pulls you away from where you need to focus.

No is a complete sentence. Don't give long reasons and excuses. It weakens your power. Just say no.

FACING LIFE'S PLATEAUS

Recently, I was talking to a young woman in New York who is building her career. She confided in me that she loved her team but she had started to feel like "the smartest person in the room," and was worried she was no longer challenged or pushed to make it to the next level.

Wow, could I relate. I told her that throughout my life and career I had these same feelings. I started to describe these times when I felt like I was standing on a plateau and bored with the status quo. Sure, it was comfortable, but it gets to be stifling.

These are the times that if you stop and think about it, you are about to grow. If you are willing to take the next leap of faith, interesting and exciting things are around the corner. Sometimes this means that you have to surround yourself with new, fascinating people who can help you grow and learn. Other times it means you have to challenge everyone around you to step up with you.

Yes, it can be a bit scary, but what if you don't take the risk to be a bigger, better you? You will never know unless you are willing to walk through the fog for a while until you see the light of a new day.

Rely on our cowgirl role models—just think of them. Cowgirls think big. What have you got to lose?!

WHEN YOU FAIL, WATCH WHO HAS YOUR BACK

Condoleezza Rice once said, "When I talk to students—and I still think of myself more than anything as a kind of professor on leave—they say, 'Well, how do I get to do what you do?' . . . And I say, 'Well, you have to start out by being a failed piano major.' And my point to them is don't try to have a ten-year plan. Find the next thing that interests you and follow that."[22]

If you are out there in the world making things happen and enjoying your power, you will face failure. It happens. Failure is the downside of risk. I always tried to minimize the impact of failure and climb back on. Deal with it and move on.

But watch who has your back. If something bad happened to us at T3, a few people would always stick their heads in my office and check on me. If we needed to talk through tough issues, they would always stay late. If we needed to make tough decisions, they provided insight and good counsel. They never let their emotions cloud a good decision.

They never overreacted or underreacted. They were grown-ups and I appreciated and valued their support. Thankfully, most of those people are still with me today. These are the wonderful people who have built their own power and know exactly how to use it to celebrate the good things and help us all through the inevitable challenges.

Once I was in a board meeting of an organization where I served as the chairman. On one particular day, one of the participants decided to challenge me. She hurled accusations and assumptions about my point of view that were both unfounded and vitriolic. In the heat of the moment I was dumbfounded, but actually held myself in check for a moment because I didn't want to lose control in front of the entire group. The immediate reaction would have been to try to dispel her comments, snap right back at her, and get the upper hand.

However, my inner cowgirl said silence is golden. And, to my delight and surprise, I didn't have to say a word. Another person in the meeting took on my accuser and put her in her place for being so outrageous. In that moment, I felt incredibly powerful, because I had gained the respect and trust of another team member. And that wonderful person had my back. Believe me, I will have that saint's back too from now on! And anyone else who is falsely blamed for anything.

Who has your back?

Think about who these people are in your life. Go give them a hug or call them on the phone. Right now.

When a cowgirl gets thrown in the rodeo arena and breaks her leg, she already knows who will run in, pick her up, and carry her out while the crowd applauds.

Lessons Learned: Cowgirls Are Fearless Leaders

- Women typically have different ways of leading than men. Women listen past words and discover unspoken emotions. Women see around corners. They are the glue that builds great teams, and that is many times more important to women who do not seek to lead from the top of a corporate hierarchy.
- Embrace change, although it can be hard. It is where you will find the biggest opportunities. Don't fear failure; it is a crucial part of learning, building confidence, and your long-term success.
- Stop and take time every now and then to do nothing or something rote and simple to give your mind a break from overstimulation and the stress of trying to excel.
- Always connect people in helpful ways. Expect nothing in return. It will make your heart full and your days filled with meaning.

Cowgirls at British exhibition in 1924
(Brooke/Stringer/Getty Images)

Chapter 11

COWGIRLS ARE DOING JUST FINE

Let's dial back to 1924 and see our fine cowgirls lined up at the British Empire Exhibition in London. Cowgirls, including Mabel Strickland, Bonnie McCarroll, Fox Hastings, and Tad Lucas to name a few, were right in the thick of things. These cowgirls were talented athletes and strong individuals but they were also part of a tight-knit team of women who cared about and supported each other. They helped each other put together better performances, and some married the brothers of other cowgirls. They took care of each other's children and nursed each other back to health when things went awry in the arena.

The exhibition in London was the largest show of its kind ever held, with British royalty in attendance. In addition to the American cowgirls and cowboys, fifty-six nations of the British Commonwealth and Empire were represented. The purpose was to stimulate trade, strengthen bonds with the mother country, and bring closer contact with one another.

Mabel and Bonnie did more than just show up. They took home the Lord Selfridge World Championship Trophy. Cowgirls were doing just fine then and today.

Through the years I have had and still have so many wonderful friends. They are true treasures in life. Count each of your friends as a precious gem, just like the cowgirls did on the rodeo circuit. "Got your backers" is what we call them at T3.

Ann Dennison Normand has been more than a friend all of my life. She is a wonderful sister in every sense of the word. Ann has been with me through each tough time in my life and is always there to celebrate the victories. Educated as a teacher, Ann later went back to school and became an Episcopalian priest. As one of the first women to take on this role, she eventually became the canon to the bishop in Texas. In business terms, it would be like a chief operating officer. She still travels with the archbishop of Canterbury and recently spent an afternoon with the pope.

Ann and I laugh at all of the things we have accomplished, each step of the way, cheering each other on. Recently, I cheered at her wedding ceremony to an Episcopalian Bishop as she started another new chapter in her life. The Reverend Dr. Ann Dennison Normand is a cowgirl, and I have photos of her in her full priest regalia on horseback to prove it!

Cowgirls find their place in life, whether performing for royalty, visiting with the pope, or sitting on the back porch watching a sunset. They take control, make good judgment calls, and take responsibility for themselves. They understand when to push and when to let go. They understand the ebb and flow of life. They get it. They make things work. They stay positive. And, most important, they stay true to who they really are. And, for a cowgirl, nothing is more important.

COWGIRL POWER

Cowgirl power is a mind-set, a big idea that can help women in business today think about their roles, decisions, and careers in different ways. Cowgirls take responsibility for themselves and set new rules. We can create our own programs, find new ways to work, build lifelong relationships, and find meaning and satisfaction in our work.

As I began to understand and take control of my personal power, I learned to wield it for the benefit of others. Build your personal power so that you can begin the good work of empowering others. Leading by the empowerment of others is a stunning accomplishment. Your power can be the source of power for hundreds of others. Those hundreds can enable thousands to grow and be empowered.

Cowgirl power is there for you. There are no limits to it. I know you can redefine personal power in ways that empower you every day to give you much more control over your own life.

GO FIND THE COWGIRLS

Look through your organization and find the cowgirls. I know they are there. Think about congratulating them for what they do. Encourage them to steal some of your power. Then get the hell out of the way! You can improve your culture, your product, your engagement levels, and your retention rates. Call me and thank me as soon as you get it done!

THANK YOU FROM THE BOTTOM OF MY HEART

There is a saying in Texas that the best sermons are lived, not preached. I hope I have not preached too much. I'm passionate about women and business because I've lived it. I know what is possible. And I know what a wonderful gift a successful career can be personally and for your family. Find your own path. It is uniquely yours, but it is there if you open your mind and heart and begin the journey.

Here's the bottom line. Be bold. Get out there. Kick some ass. And, as you do it, build buckets and buckets of goodwill as you go. Treat people well, do favors, and help their kids. Do the right thing and it all comes around. You make your own luck. Give a helping hand to good people who need it. Cowgirls have faith in the way things turn out if they approach life with a big heart. And cowgirls are usually right.

And go to gaygaddis.com and tell me about how you did it so I can share with my readers what we all can learn. Oh, and please share your tamale stories!

Climb on, cowgirl, and ride.

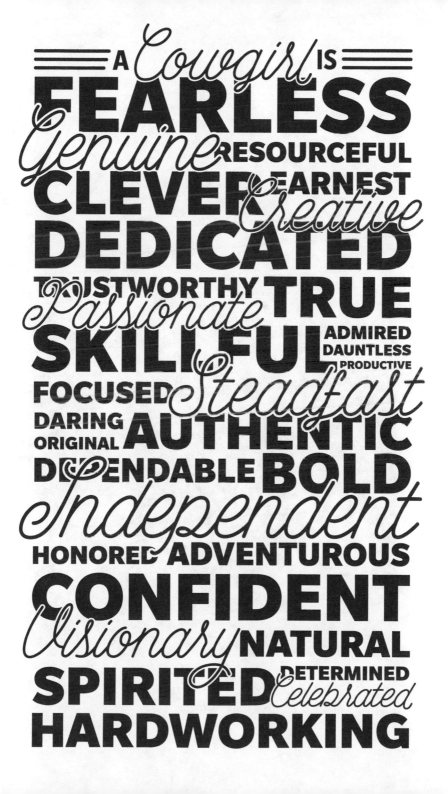

Mamie Francis Hafley with Napoleon
*(Accession Number RC2006.076.228 © Dickinson Research Center,
National Cowboy & Western Heritage Museum, Oklahoma City, Oklahoma)*

Cowgirl Power Toolkit

You can clearly see that Mamie Francis Hafley had a few tricks up her sleeve to help her power through life. Here she is hamming it up with her faithful friend and steed, Napoleon.

Mamie knew how to thrill audiences and had a horse diving act riding off a fifty-foot-high platform into a barrel of water just ten feet across! Between 1908 and 1914 she performed this stunt 628 times. The fact that she couldn't swim never stopped her!

She also performed as a sharpshooter, and did her rifle shooting from horseback in Wild West shows. Francis was teamed with Princess Winona in a vaudeville-shooting act known as Winona and Francis. Always drawing on her toolkit of experience and lessons learned, she continued to re-create herself and her performances throughout her life.[23]

This is my "Cowgirl Power Toolkit." It is based on my life experiences that I described throughout the book. The toolkit contains easy-to-read, quick summaries of all of the main ideas in the book for easy reference. These are some of the sources of positive personal power. They are limitless and are available to everyone. I'm sure there are many more than I describe here. We will each find our own unique sources. These sources of power are not bestowed on you. Some you earn, some you adopt because they speak to you, some are inspirational directions.

Read through the ideas and pick two or three that are interesting to you. Then begin to apply them and practice at purposefully getting better at them. Think about ways you can stand out, inspire people, and build your power. The good news is that you don't have to attend a conference or go to a seminar or endure an in-house training session to learn these techniques.

Think about these different approaches from a long-term perspective. How could implementing a few of these impact your family and your career in five years? Or twenty? How could these ideas help your children have happy, successful lives?

How can you string some of these ideas together? If you want to be a better public speaker but you are not super confident, add a serving of self-deprecating humor to your opening remarks. You'll be fine. You will see lots of opportunity to mix and match the recommendations.

Work with your confidants, the Rough Riders. Experiment with this in the safety of that close-knit group of trusted advisors. Talk to your friends and co-workers about these ideas over lunch. Share information about what works and does not work for each of you. The more you make this tangible, the more effective it will be for you. Practice, practice, practice.

I sincerely believe that if we all change the discourse and stop focusing on our lack of power and instead focus on building our own personal power, we can change the realities of our lives for the better. We can show our children pathways to success. We can live happier, more fulfilling lives.

The toolkit is a working, living document. It has more ideas than I was able to cover in the book.

Cowgirls Are Responsible for Themselves

Cowgirls are taught at an early age to be responsible for themselves. They are expected to have both good judgment and self-control. It is critical that you take full responsibility for yourself. Don't blame someone else, that is not the cowgirl way.

Here are a few helpful ideas.

The Dreams and Reality Exercise

Let yourself go and write down your dreams. Who do you want to be? What do you want to accomplish? Who do you want to inspire? Where will you be happy? Where will you be satisfied with your life?

Then write down the reality of who and where you are today. Be completely honest. If it is good, face it head-on. If it is bad, face it head-on. The ability to see yourself from afar is profound and invaluable on the road to success.

Now begin to connect the dots that will take you from today's reality to tomorrow's dream. Don't get too granular yet, look for directions and pathways. If a path is closed, find a way around. Work on it. Pathways will begin to emerge. They will require lots of work and effort, but they are there. Not all of them will take you to a good place. But each path you follow will help you grow.

Set Your Goals, Do It Again, and Again

After you identify pathways, focus on goals. Pathways are not prescriptive. They are directional, like compass settings. They are not a road map. Setting goals begins to build your road map. Goals are about what you are going to do to follow a pathway. Write them down. Make them tangible. Save them so you can measure your progress.

Supercharge your goals by sharing them. Talk about them. Be accountable for reaching them. Do not just write them down on a yellow pad and put them in a desk drawer. There is nothing more awesome than achieving a goal and checking it off your list.

Who has shared their goals with you? Why? Why not?

Meet People Where They Are

Believe in your heart that each person you meet in life has a piece of your own life puzzle. Believe that you have a piece of that person's puzzle to share with them. Approach them with that mind-set—with a sincere desire to put all the pieces together. It will profoundly change the way you relate to people and how they will relate to you.

When you meet people, invest a little time and energy so

that both of you can understand which puzzle pieces may fit together.

Ride High in the Saddle

Don't try to wear someone else's hat. You will never be happy doing that. An attorney once told me, "I don't feel confident when I go into a room in flats because I'm short. I always bring a pair of high heels to change into." Put on those heels and stand tall. Do what works for you.

We all have different needs, uncertainties, and fears. Understand them, own them, and be in control of yourself. That is where you find your power.

Build Your Own Brand

Stand for something. Be interesting. Give people a reason to reach out to you, to connect to you. Find a style, a look that is uniquely yours. Find an interesting, engaging way to meet people. Be quirky and original.

I had a guy who worked for me who had a very dapper sense of style and usually wore a bow tie. He always told me, "You should dress like you give a shit."

Build Your Rough Rider Team

Take responsibility to be sure you are getting feedback. Find a few teammates or friends who agree to give you candid feedback. Do the same for them. Feedback is invaluable because it is how we learn to perfect our skills. We all get too little of it.

Find people who will tell you the truth—who will tell you if you are "up talking" or using a singsong voice. Those who will tell you that you are on the wrong path.

Do the same for them. Be candid about both the good and bad. You will both grow more powerful together.

Try Saying Yes

Open your mind to opportunity. Say yes to the good things that come your way. How do you know which opportunities are the good ones? If they are a little scary or will make you stretch beyond what you are comfortable with today, then they are the good ones. Achieving success is never a straight line, it twists and turns and presents itself unclearly and unexpectedly.

Go say yes to the right things. Make your own luck. If you say yes to the wrong thing, fail fast and shut it down. That is a very powerful thing to do.

What Makes You Authentic?

The dreams and reality exercise asks you to be honest with yourself about your current reality. When you do that you quickly come to the question "Who am I?" When you answer that question, focus on what you do well because that is where your authenticity lives.

Focus on building on those truths about you that make you proud. Work on making those truths more accessible to you and your friends and family. This is not about building perception.

Deliver the truth about who you are every day.

Hang Out with People Who Pull You Forward

If you have ambition and want to succeed, spend your time with people who can and will pull you forward with them. Evaluate everyone you come into contact with against this measure. It works both ways, look for people who you can pull forward. If you have friends or family that do not measure up, be nice to them but don't overinvest.

Think of all the people you know as a portfolio of access to success and personal power. Invest wisely.

Stop and Kiss the Clown

When you see someone who has excelled, made an extra effort, or who is an unsung hero, stand up and recognize them. Find the right moment to do it, but make a point of publicly saying thank you. You'll make someone's day. You'll put some goodwill into those buckets of yours. And it will power you up because no one else thought to do it.

Cowgirls Build Their Own Competence

You have to do the work to build your competence. You have to build your skills and knowledge. Competence is not bestowed on you. You don't wake up one day and decide you are competent. You earn it. If you want to be a respected team member, you have to earn that respect. Be curious, a self-learner, a self-starter.

Be All In at Work

The truth is that many people live in a fog at work. It is startling, but a fact. Too many people are simply not engaged with their work because they do not care. That is the saddest thing in the world.

People who love what they do are highly engaged. I call it "being all in." These are the people who make magic. It is inspiring, highly contagious, and empowers us all.

Be all in and watch who follows you.

What Do You Do Better Than Anyone Else?

Think about it. Maybe you are not better than anyone else today. But where are you closest? Where are you competitive? Figure this out and put most of your energy there.

Women tend to have too much self-doubt. I know a young woman in high school who was struggling with physics and asked for help from a friend. She later learned that she got an A in the course and he got a B. She had actually mastered the coursework better than him. Her confidence had not caught up with her ability.

If you were to ask me what I do better than anyone else today, I would say that I am a Master Connector of People. Am I really the best? I'm not sure, but I believe I'm damn competitive at the game.

You are better than you think you are.

Where Do You Suck?

This is the flip side of the "what do you do better" question. Where do you suck? Understanding the answer to both of these questions is part of the reality exercise. And it is one of the most liberating things you can do for yourself.

I am not a detail person. I try to write down the details. I make all kinds of lists, but then I misplace them and feel guilty and ashamed. The good news is that I always remember the big issues. But I suck at even finding those lists, much less executing them. As my dad once said, "You can't find your butt with both hands." Whew!

When I finally realized that, I let it go. It was one of the happiest days of my life. I stopped pretending to even deal with the details. I felt powerful enough to start each meeting with a pronouncement about my weakness and ask who in the group would keep track of the details. And, who would promise to be able to find that list tomorrow?

I'm now working on my next biggest weakness. It has something to do with shoes.

Study Personality Type

Understand the basics of personality types. Learn to see introversion and extraversion. Learn the difference between thinking and judging. Just knowing that people can see the exact same thing in radically different ways is powerful. You do not need to be an expert, just be aware of its importance.

If it interests you, take one of the personality tests. It is more helpful and fun if you do it with your teammates, friends, or family so you can compare and talk about it. If you are still interested, read some books or take a class or two. If you are going to be dealing with people in your career, this is the secret sauce to your personal power.

Some people see trees. Some people see forests. Helping them see each other is powerful stuff.

Don't Ask for Permission

Cowgirls don't cotton too much to others lording authority over them. When the circus comes to town, they might just join the show and be gone the next day. A little town in Nebraska today, Madison Square Garden tomorrow. Cowgirls are bold. They can be impulsive. They have confidence in their gut and are not afraid to take a risk to be a star.

Ask for forgiveness later.

Charity Can Take You a Long Way

Do good things—for yourself and others. Working with non-profits is good work that helps others. But as you build your competence, nonprofits give you a great place to exercise your growing cowgirl power in a safe, supportive environment. The people around you in these organizations share your values and goals. They will support you and not let you fail. Be bold here. Take risks. Then apply what you have learned to both your personal life and career.

Do good for others, and yourself.

Make Your Own Luck

Life is like a pinball machine. The more you play, the higher your score will be. You never know where things will go and how they will work out. But you should know with certainty that the harder you play at making connections, learning, and leading with your heart the luckier you will be.

Be curious. Ask questions. Look around the corners. It is OK to even be a little pesky. Go for it, all they can do is run you off.

Always Have a Point of View

Most women I know shy away from debates and confrontations. Debate class was one of the best life lessons I ever learned. You have to debate issues because if you don't, you will never have a strong point of view. If you do not advocate for a position and allow yourself to be challenged, you will not have thought through all the implications. And you won't be very interesting.

Get a nice bottle of wine and a good friend and respectfully go argue with each other.

Cowgirls Use Their Competence to Find Assertiveness

I see women trying to become more assertive. They read articles that give them all kinds of advice, most of which is bullshit. The truth is you cannot be authentically assertive without having built your own competence. But when you have done the work, you have earned the right to be authentically assertive. You have the right to be heard, because you have something important and interesting to say.

Know How to Be Assertive and Win

Cowgirls know that on the ranch and in board of directors meetings that women can come across as being too aggressive. Cowgirls have earned the right to be heard, and when they want to make a point, they stand up and express themselves boldly, taking on a bit of masculine persona. They speak their mind without fear of being judged.

But they also know when to shut up. They follow up with a little humor. They ask questions. They are open-minded. And they listen carefully, now switching to a more feminine approach.

This double whammy of boldness followed by an open and friendly demeanor eliminates the risk of being bitchy. Cowgirls know how to do it instinctively. They have been leading cowboys around by the nose since the beginning of time.

Women who learn how to do this with confidence and ease actually can come across as more powerful than most men. It is a wonderfully unfair advantage because men can't do it.

Express yourself boldly, smile, and sit down.

Listen to Your Gut

Your gut is your guide to assertiveness. Your gut is a combination of dreams, reality, experiences, fears, and doubts. Your gut is the summation of who you are. When you need to take a stand, be bold, and speak your mind, check your gut first. While it is usually a bit vague and rarely logical, listen carefully.

When your gut speaks to you, pay close attention. Even if your mind says it is a risky move, if your gut says go for it, be decisive, be bold, and go for it.

Your gut will rarely steer you wrong.

That Last Item on Your Checklist

There is power in that checklist. When it gets too long it can be daunting. But when you whittle it down and before you go to bed, check off the last item; there is a huge sense of accomplishment and power that keeps you warm and snuggly all night.

It is the things I have not resolved that keep me up all night. Some of those you have to let go. As Scarlett O'Hara said, "I can't think about this now. I'll go crazy if I do. I'll think about it tomorrow." Having a lot on your plate demonstrates your value and your personal power. Do what you can do today.

Then check that off of that list with joy and satisfaction. Sleep tight.

Understand the Money

I asked a young professional woman about how she built her confidence. I was surprised when she told me that her therapist had encouraged her to understand how her employer made money. She took a deep dive and quickly learned how her job contributed to the company's overall financial success.

"Suddenly a lot of fuzzy issues about my career became crystal clear. It all fell in place. I am so much more comfortable," she said. I like this a lot. Understanding the money is fundamental to being positively assertive.

So forget the therapist and invite the CFO out to lunch.

Be a Storyteller

Cowgirls grow up learning a powerful skill, storytelling. Their grandparents, aunts, and uncles all have stories that come down through the generations. They are full of lessons on values, character, and courage. They are stories full of danger and life-changing dramatic events. And all of them have twists of irony, humor, and love.

Storytelling is an incredible source of personal power. In fact, most great leaders are amazing storytellers. Storytelling enables you to advocate for an issue by stringing together all of the arguments, both pro and con, but to do it in an engaging, entertaining way. Storytelling is a way to teach values, vision, and culture by explaining their origin.

Cowgirls sit together with their peers, friends, and families and tell stories around a campfire that inspire us all. Learn the art of storytelling. Think about the lessons you want to teach. Make them authentic.

Speak from Your Heart

Whether you are telling stories around a campfire or standing in front of an audience of a thousand people, there will come a moment when you want to make an important point—to tell a truth. When this moment comes, step away from the podium and speak from the bottom of your heart. Let your emotions go; don't be afraid of them.

When you speak from your heart, it puts people on the edge of their seats. Why? Because they don't hear it very often. Open with a laugh. Close with a heartfelt truth.

The Blue Goofus

My dad used to talk about getting the Blue Goofus. He would get restless, uneasy, and kind of grumpy. We all get in the dumps every now and then. He taught me that the best thing to do when the Blue Goofus shows up is to smile at it and tell it hello, to acknowledge it and try to figure out what is going on. Usually, it means something is wrong, out of whack. Or that there is a big change coming that will have to be dealt with.

When the Blue Goofus shows up, don't avoid it. Go sit by it and hold its hand. You'll figure it out.

Earn Trust

There is nothing more powerful and enduring than earning trust. My business is totally based on trust. We have done business with so many people through the years, and we have earned their trust by simply doing what we say we will do. It takes time and effort. Step by step. Slow by slow. Nothing, absolutely nothing, is more valuable.

I have people who have worked for me for years who I trust blindly.

Who do you trust? Who trusts you blindly?

Acts of Profound Kindness

We send little red cowboy boots to all of our employees, clients, and partners who have newborns. At first, we just thought it was a nice thing to do. Over the past twenty years and hundreds of red boots later, it has come to mean something much more. I now see it as a signal that we send to new parents that we value them and are proud to be a part of their lives and their families. Almost without exception, at about eighteen months each of those babies walk in our office proudly wearing their red boots. When those parents take the time to walk those children in to see us, it is the most profound act of kindness I ever receive.

Are you as kind as you want to be?

Solve a Problem

Earning the right to be assertive is a fundamental source of personal power. The path to earning that right is solving problems. There are always problems. And there are always plenty of people who are eager to point them out. But the people who apply themselves to find creative solutions are the powerful ones. They research the issues, apply analytical discipline, and then build consensus for the solution. They teach everyone how to approach problems. They teach people how to work together to improve.

Real problem solvers are the high priests of the business world. Bless you.

Sometimes You Have to Push Yourself

It is not all roses and bluebirds out there. There are times when you need to reach down into your gut and find the power to push yourself forward to success. Sometimes it requires an all-nighter, or a weekend of work. Sometimes it means another sales call at the end of a long day. Sometimes it means having to deal with a difficult situation.

Put your head down and power through it. Be strong. And, each time you do it, it will get a little easier. Each time you do it, if you look behind you, you will see more people following you. More people who have your back.

Power through. It will make you stronger. And more respected and admired.

Design Your Own Life

Most young mothers that I know tend to live in the moment, emotionally engaged with their children in the here and now. They focus entirely on their young children and, often, do not think about themselves. That is fine, it is usually the right thing to do. But stop and do this next exercise. It is the right thing to do for your family and, most importantly, for yourself.

Timeline Your Life

Sit down and build a timeline for your life. Map out the coming years and who and where everyone will be. Of course you cannot see into the future. But a lot is knowable and when you put it on a timeline, it becomes a more seeable sequence of events.

When do the kids go to college? How old will you be? How does the money work? Do you love your work? If not, when could you make a change? Where will you be in your career when that happens? How are you going to pay for their education? Can you give your children more opportunities if you make an important decision now? Would a job change or a move to another city radically improve your collective lives? When will you need to take care of your own parents? When do grandchildren come?

Sketch it out on a big sheet of paper. Identify and circle the big changes you know are coming. These are intersections of opportunity to change course or double down. This is a work in progress, so just sketch out ideas. Don't try to finish it.

As you sketch it out, issues, ideas, and opportunities will emerge. Ask yourself, what can I do now in my career that will dramatically improve our family's life fifteen years from now? What lessons can I teach my children about values?

Then share the timeline with your spouse. Adjust and spend a couple of weeks talking about it.

Then show it to your kids. Talk about it. Ask their opinions. Start the dialogue. Find ways to include some of their ideas. Give them the gift of knowing more about where they are going than they do now. Tell them it will not be perfect. Tell them that based on what you know right now, this is the direction we want to follow. There is immense power in this dialogue.

Start on this right now.

What Matters Right Now

As you build your timeline it will be clear what matters right now, and that is where you should focus most of your effort. Take care of what matters right now. Be all in. Focus on now, but keep glancing into the future when you have a little time. Be present. Be there for your kids, your partner, and your teammates. There is no greater gift that you can give.

When you come to important milestones, pull out the timeline and show everyone, including yourself, where you are. When you make big changes in your life, pull it out and explain why you chose a new path.

It helps everyone to know where you are.

Who Takes Care of the Kids?

If you are old enough to remember, this is the $64,000 question. If you are not, go look it up.

The answer is that if you both have rewarding careers and good earning potential, you can figure it out. It requires imagination and grit. It means spending too much money on childcare, but if you look at long-term earning potential for you both and careers that you both love, I believe you can make it work.

If not, it comes down to who makes the most money. Take the ego and gender issues out of the decision and make a good family business decision. I know lots of women who have had powerful careers and made it into the C-suite or built their own successful companies. Many of them had stay-at-home husbands who were very supportive of their careers. Many of them have part-time careers that they return to when the kids are gone. And, I have to say, they are happily married and confident they made the right decisions.

Make a good business decision.

Let's Dispense with the Guilt

Children of working parents turn out fine. In fact, there is new research from Harvard that working moms should not feel guilty about going to work. If anything, they are doing things that benefit their children.[24] Children of working parents, especially working professionals, get great exposure to interesting people, ideas, and opportunities as a result of their parents' careers.

So let's just hang up guilt in the barn and let it dry.

Don't Separate Work from Family

Find ways to bring work into your family life and your family into your work. Celebrate work successes with your kids, even if they do not fully understand. If you had a hard day at work, tell your kids when you get home. They will find a way to cheer you up. Separating work from family is not good for anyone because it creates unnatural vacuums of information in both directions. Bring them to work and let them run around and scream every now and then.

Do not allow work and family to be two different things.

Stay in the Game

If you have a promising career, stay in the game whether you work full-time or stay at home with the kids. Freelance, network, work part-time, consult. Keep your skills and knowledge well honed so that when the kids are gone, you have lots and lots of great options.

Fight like hell to stay current, relevant, interesting, and connected.

You Have to Have Help

If you want a family and a career, you have to be honest with yourself that you cannot do it all. You have to have help. There are all kinds of ways to do it. We have encouraged young mothers to bring their babies to work at T3. We will have had well over one hundred children in the program by the time this book is published.

You probably do not have access to a program like ours, but reach out and build a support network. You will go crazy if you don't.

The Path to Success Is Not a Straight Line

Life does not present itself in a well-organized, logical way. Problems and opportunities come at you on their own schedule. You can affect some of it, but certainly not all. One thing leads to another. And to another. And to another. It is much like playing pinball. But pay attention: Each time that bell goes off and a light flashes, dig deeper because each hit is probably an opportunity if you see it in the right light.

Go with your gut and follow the interesting opportunities, and look for new connections every step of the way. Weave them together in creative, openhearted ways, and go build a successful life.

Cowgirls Build a Kick-Ass Culture

I love the quote "Culture eats strategy for breakfast." There seems to be a lot of confusion about its real origin, so I'll just acknowledge that it is not mine. But it has certainly been my experience. We have ups and downs with our culture. Sometimes we hit rocky times and things were not great. Sometimes we made a bad hire. But when those storm clouds blew in, we always saw it quickly and tried to resolve it quickly because I believe a business's culture is everything.

Become a Cultural Missionary

A company's culture is about values, about how you treat people, about what you believe. Culture is about long-lived tradition. Own your culture. Provide empathy. Provide compassion. Have high expectations. Demand results.

Regardless of your position of authority or lack of authority, take ownership of culture. Become a missionary. Build on the good things. Protect the values.

Show people your authentic love of your company's culture. If you do, your power soars.

Why You Are Obligated to Disagree

The power of truth is startling. If you hear something you disagree with, you are obligated to speak out. If you don't, your team loses the opportunity to learn something.

If you do not, you open the door to passive-aggressive behavior, which means negative undercurrents exist without you talking about them. Have the guts and grit to ferret out passive-aggressive behavior. The only thing worse is an asshole.

You know when someone is holding back. Don't allow it.

What Do You Think?

We do a lot of conference calls in our business. After we hang up, we immediately call our team members back for a quick regroup. We always open that second call with the question addressed to one of the newest, least experienced team members, "What did you think?" It's a sink or swim moment, because the newbie is put on the spot. How they react tells you volumes, and I am usually impressed. If the answer is not insightful, then the entire team immediately knows what knowledge gaps need to be filled. If the response is insightful, the entire team wins. The new member is rewarded with respect and their trust goes up.

Ask the newbie what they think. You might be surprised.

Grab Smart People Around the Neck

Beware of people who are intimidated by people smarter than themselves. They are the second most dangerous people in an organization, right behind assholes. People who are intimidated by smart people instinctively hire less capable people because they worry about being upstaged. Left unchecked, someone in a hiring position who lacks the self-confidence of dealing with smart people will dumb down an organization. I have seen people actually hide résumés of people who scared them.

Never fear hiring people more capable than you. That is the definition of success in business. Hire smart, talented people, and all the boats rise.

Gay's Rules of Order for Effective Meetings

I believe more than half of the challenges that women face at work are a result of a lack of guiding principles in their workplace —especially around team conduct. Here are my rules on how teams interact:

- You have an obligation to participate. If you don't you will not be invited back.
- You have an obligation to be heard. You were invited because we thought you had something to contribute. If someone tries to dominate the conversation, swat them down.
- You have an obligation to be respectful of team members. Be all in, not on your cell phone or laptop. Meetings start and end on time, agendas are published in advance, and clear assignments are made.

- You have an obligation to be blunt, truthful, and brave. If this is a shit show project, just say so. Trust the team to fix it.
- You have an obligation to have a point of view and advocate it.
- You have an obligation to disagree. You were not invited to sit there like a lump.
- You have an obligation to be nice to ideas. Collect ideas without judgment, then come back with each team member having a vote and prioritize the best collective ideas.
- You have an obligation to be sure that diverse points of view are heard.
- You have an obligation to spend a few minutes before or after each meeting to say hello to your team members and ask about their family, dogs, and interests.
- You have an obligation to run assholes away.

Follow my Rules of Order, and a lot of your problems will go away. If you have an obligation to participate, you cannot be offended by the microaggression of not being asked. Buck up and speak! I believe it is usually good to have a specific team leader that moderates discussions, but that does not absolve other team members of holding everyone accountable to the rules.

Mentorship Is Great, But Lack of One Is No Excuse

I am afraid that a lack of a good mentor is too often used as an excuse for why women do not excel in business. Women need mentors and men do not? Really! Do not sit around and wait for a mentor to magically show up. Own your own success. I have had five mentors in my career; that is one about every six years. You will be lucky if you encounter two or three.

However, when one appears in your life, seize the opportunity and make it a great experience for both of you. Having a mentor who is willing to spend time with you is a validation of your competence. If you had not already done the hard work and built your knowledge and skills, the mentor would not waste their time on you. Take it as a compliment and work hard to give back to your mentor more than you take.

Whom will you mentor next?

Have High Expectations for Your Boss

Much of what people hope for from a mentor should actually come from their boss, supervisor, or team leader. It's called leadership. Leaders are paid to lead and they should be accountable. Mentors are occasional volunteers. Leaders are a scalable resource. Mentors are not.

Have high expectations of your boss and take equal responsibility for the relationship. Be engaging and inspirational. Find a way to help. Raise your hand for the tough projects. Become a most valuable player.

Help your boss be better.

Be Kind, Not Nice

Confront problems head-on. Deal with them and make sure everyone learns from them. Not confronting issues is kind, but not nice. You are not doing anyone a favor by not confronting problems—and what's worse is that you often will cause harm to the overall emotional health of the team.

No one has ever called me nice.

Shoot the Assholes

Your personal power depends on your willingness to draw a line in the sand. It is your responsibility to maintain a positive, healthy environment. If you have someone who is negatively impacting your team, you have a responsibility to intervene and try to resolve the issue. But if that does not work, you have an obligation to shoot the asshole. Negative energy drains team spirit; it is a dark rain cloud that does not go away.

Never tolerate an asshole.

Cowgirls Know a Good Idea When They See One

We work together because collectively we are better than when we work individually. Ideas need to be managed with respect, openness, and open debate.

Constant Forward Motion

Our mantra at T3 is the idea of "constant forward motion." We continually ask ourselves to gain forward motion in all things. Where can we improve? What expertise do we need to add? What capabilities do we develop next? Constant forward motion is about the big stuff. And the very small stuff.

Ask yourself. Ask your teams for specific examples of how you have moved your organization forward. Do it every month. Then every week. Then every day. Do it often enough and it becomes an organizational instinct.

Great Things Start as a Few Small Things

Virtually everything is an opportunity. It may look like a problem, and it may be. But usually behind that problem is a tiny little opportunity to improve. Learn to see the world from this perspective. Always, always look for the upside in everything and believe that each little thing can be put together in ways that become wonderful things.

This is powerful stuff. It's one part curiosity and one part optimism. I have seen us take a simple idea like the house slippers we created for UPS and turn it into a multimillion-dollar business.

Our Four-Step Process

Our culture has evolved to cherish, protect, and enhance ideas. We basically have four steps:

- Generating free-form ideas—nothing is rejected
- Building on the ideas, mixing, linking, twisting them
- Evaluating which ideas are the best ways to solve the problem at hand
- Determining which of those ideas have the potential to be a platform

Learn to Use Straw Dogs

Success is not always a straight line. The solution to a problem or opportunity is often not clear. Real leaders understand how to work through this.

When you face ambiguity, when the path forward is not clear, the best way forward is with straw dogs. You come up with a potential solution to the problem—it can be thoughtful and compelling, or it can be funny and whimsical. It does not matter. Ask everyone on the team for their straw dogs. It is OK because they are just straw and no one is going to get hurt.

What you will see is that people will start shooting at some of the dogs and others will be left standing. Do it over and over again, and the solution will emerge. When you are looking at a blank whiteboard, you have nothing to react to and people get stuck. They are invaluable because they give the team something to react to. Reacting to a vacuum does not provide much insight. Put up straw dogs, shoot some down, and the ones left standing are potential solutions to the problem.

Put up some straw dogs today.

Gay's Rules on Developing Ideas

Managing ideas requires laying down some cultural principles, some ground rules. These are the steps to developing ideas.

- Fear goes out the window
- Big ideas come from small ideas, start with curiosity
- The team owns the idea, individuals do not
- Ideas are never judged, until later
- It is fine to build one on top of another
- Argue for an idea. Conflict is an important part of the process
- Take a break, get away from it

- As a group, pick the top three
- Prototype each one as fast as you can
- Release it in a safe zone
- Tweak it some, iterate, iterate
- Let it go
- Ask "What do you think?" but don't answer with "I think." Start your response with a positive, forceful statement.

Put 'Em Up on the Wall

When it is time to begin evaluating the ideas, put them up on the wall and discuss them. See what resonates. Look for opportunities to build on them. Then ask everyone to vote on the best ones using colored stickers. No discussion should be allowed during this step. Then evaluate and iterate and keep going until you are done.

By the way, this is an incredible exercise to teach your kids how to work as a team!

The Power of Three Workable Ideas

Pick the top contenders and debate the merits of each. Narrow them down to three different ideas everyone would be comfortable presenting to the client. This requires real thoughtfulness. You are about to release the ideas into the wild. Never include one you do not believe in, because without fail, that is the one that will get selected.

Let the best idea win.

Make It. Don't Talk About It.

Instead of starting new projects with written proposals, elaborate project plans, and detailed estimates, go prototype it. Just go make it. Don't talk about it. Just do it. This focus on action and making changed my business. We are often able to put our ideas in the hands of our clients and show them how it actually works. We get amazing reactions because they can see the power of it, even if it is not perfectly designed and executed yet. Powerful stuff.

Prototype. Don't pontificate.

In Search of the Adjacent Possible—Find Big Ideas

In the business world an adjacent possible is something that was not apparent before, but suddenly emerges and can be combined with another element to create something entirely new. The classic example is when Johannes Gutenberg in the fifteenth century took existing ideas like movable type, ink, paper, and the concept of a press (for making wine) and put them together and built something that never existed before: the first printing press.

Look for new ways to combine ideas. Teach your teams to mash up different technologies. Be creative and look beyond the obvious. Ideas come from curiosity.

One of our executives at T3 told me that she wakes up every morning curious. And that is a wonderful thing. Shouldn't we all?

Cowgirls Are Fearless Leaders

We need women in leadership positions. You may not be in line for the C-suite just yet, but there are skills you can work on now that will prepare you for when those opportunities present themselves.

Be All In

To take a leadership role on a team, in your own business, or in the C-suite, you have to have the mentality of being "all in" the game. You have to be totally committed to actively lead with real solid conviction. You owe it to yourself and to your teams. Anything else will usually lead you into failure.

Don't accept leadership if your heart is not in it. It is not fair to anyone. Taking on a leadership role makes you responsible for the success of everyone on the team.

Do accept leadership roles if you feel a strong sense of conviction that you will lead them to a good place.

Put Yourself Out There

First and foremost, a leader has to put themselves out there. Leaders need to be accessible and visible. They need to stitch together relationships with shareholders, customers, employees, regulators, and the press. They must be great listeners because the interests of each of those groups are not always aligned. It requires constantly reaching out and really connecting.

Do Things You Have Never Done Before

At T3 we pride ourselves in doing things that have never been done before; in fact, we have been doing it for thirty years. And we rarely fail. How do we do it? We have a process and culture around breaking new ground. When we move into that mode, we understand that risk lurks everywhere. We are all on high alert. We double and triple test everything. We beat on systems to try to make them fail.

When was the last time you did something you have never done before?

Build a Network to Be Visible

As a leader your network is your pathway to success. You need to actively build it to be sure you have a big pipeline of opportunity. You need to be purposeful about those you seek to influence—are you focused on the right people? And you need to be assertive in order to be visible, to get people's attention. It takes passion, conviction, and courage. But it is one of the best rewards of leadership.

Actively, purposefully, and assertively build your network. Once you do, be visible and stay visible. Let people know what you are doing and thinking. Participate. Show up. Engage. Having a lot of contacts in your network is only the first step. Working with them and teaching them what you are interested in is what adds value.

Embrace Risk

The willingness to take risk is what moves people, teams, and organizations forward. There is very little gain without taking some risk. Leadership is all about evaluating risk versus reward. To be an effective leader you have to embrace risk and be willing to fall flat on your face. A wise leader can learn to mitigate risk and improve the odds of success.

Think about how much risk you are willing to take to move forward. Like any smart cowgirl, sometimes you start small, then increase your risk tolerance based on your skills and knowledge.

Give Your Power Away

One of the joys of leadership is to give your power away. Each time you give someone new responsibilities, you make your teams stronger, more confident, and effective. You grow your people. And, what is more important, you are able to focus on constant forward motion.

Gain power by giving some of it away.

Say No

I advocate saying yes to the right opportunities. But I also advocate saying no to things that don't matter, that are distractions. The things you say no to are often more important than your yes decisions. Be judgmental. Be protective of your time and energy.

Cut through the clutter. Focus on what matters. Don't be afraid to say no.

Make Fun of Yourself

When you develop your personal power and move into leadership positions, there are very few talents more powerful than self-deprecating humor. If you can make fun of yourself, you are demonstrating both your personal power and your self-confidence. It requires strength and courage, and people understand that. If I can kick off a speech with a good laugh, I can own the room. Don't try it if you are not in a position of strength, but if you are it is the ultimate power play.

Learn to be the butt of your own joke.

Watch for Life's Plateaus

We all reach plateaus in our life, in our work, and in our families. Maybe things are getting a little dull. Maybe systems that have worked for you for years are no longer working. Maybe your legal and financial advisors are not the best choices today.

As we mature, as we grow our businesses, as we become

more expert, we have to step up and forward. And, often, that means we have to leave some things behind. Watch for plateaus. They are usually a good sign that you are moving forward.

When You Fail, Watch Who Has Your Back

One last thought. When you fail, and you will, watch who has your back. Watch who checks up on you. Who cares about you and offers a hand up? Pay close attention because these are the people that really love you. It is important for you to understand that.

Whose back do you have?

NOTES

1 Jewelle Bickford, coalition chair, Paradigm for Parity, LLC

2 Ashley Crossman, "Power," ThoughtCo., April 15, 2016, https://www.thoughtco.com/power-p2-3026460.

3 Deborah Tedford, "Tamales for Christmas Are a True Texas Tradition," NPR, December 24, 2009, http://www.npr.org/templates/story/story.php?storyId =121791809.

4 Lisa Chadderdon, "How Dell Sells on the Web," *Fast Company*, August 31, 1998, https://www.fastcompany .com/35071/how-dell-sells-web.

5 Jim Olson, "Fox Hastings, One Tough Girl," *Cowboy Heroes!* (blog), October 9, 2014, http://mycowboyheroes.blogspot .com/2014/10/fox-hastings-one-tough-gal.html.

6 Sharmilla Ganesan, "What Do Women Leaders Have In Common?," *The Atlantic*, August 17, 2016, http://www.theatlantic.com/business/archive/2016/08/what-do-women-leaders-have-in-common/492656/.

7 Shelley Correll and Caroline Simard, "Research: Vague Feedback Is Holding Women Back," *Harvard Business Review*, April 29, 2016, https://hbr.org/2016/04/research-vague-feedback-is-holding-women-back.

8 Steve Ember and Barbara Klein, "Annie Oakley, 1860–1926: One of the Most Famous Sharpshooters in American History," ManyThings.org, http://www.manythings.org/voa/people/Annie_Oakley.html.

9 Ibid

10 Richard Hamilton, "Buffalo Bill with Annie Oakley Wild West Show," Pennsylvania State Sportsmen's Association, http://www.pssatrap.org/oakley-annie-wild-west-show/annie-oakley.htm.

11 Farrah Penn, "I Spent a Week Trying to Be a More Assertive Woman in the Workplace," *BuzzFeed*, December, 6, 2015, https://www.buzzfeed.com/farrahpenn/i-spent-a-week-trying-to-be-a-more-assertive-woman-inthe-wo?utm_term=.kkZeRzOVX#.gxOgLpwB1.

12 Marguerite Rigoglioso, "Researchers: How Women Can Succeed in the Workplace," *Insights by Stanford Business*,

March 1, 2011, https://www.gsb.stanford.edu/insights
/researchers-how-women-can-succeed-workplace.

13 Claire Cain Miller, "Mounting Evidence of Advantages
for Children of Working Mothers," *New York Times*, May
15, 2015, https://www.nytimes.com/2015/05/17
/upshot/mounting-evidence-of-some-advantages-for
-children-of-working-mothers.html.

14 Taylor Bruce, "Ruben's Drugstore Tamales," *Southern Living*, http://www.southernliving.com/travel/southwest/
rubens-drugstore-tamales-sanantonio.

15 Jim Olson, "Mabel Strickland First Lady of Rodeo," *Cowboy Heroes*, June 17, 2013, http://mycowboyheroes
.blogspot.com/2013/06/mabel-strickland.html.

16 Ibid

17 Ruth Ayers, "Champion Girl Won Fame On Reno to
New York Ride," *The Pittsburgh Press*, April 21, 1935,
https://news.google.com/newspapers?nid=1144&
dat=19350421&id=5f8cAAAAIBAJ&sjid
=n44EAAAAIBAJ&pg=2573,368109.

18 Pew Research Center, "Women and Leadership: What
Makes a Good Leader, and Does Gender Matter?," January 14, 2015, http://www.pewsocialtrends.org/2015/
01/14/chapter-2-what-makes-a-good-leader-and-does
-gender-matter/.

19 Wendy Solomon, "When Is Female Leadership an Ad-

vantage?," *Lehigh Business*, November 3, 2015, http://www1.lehigh.edu/news/when-female-leadership -advantage-0.

20 Carmina Danini, "No One Told Ford Tamales Need to Be Unwrapped," *Houston Chronicle*, December 31, 2006, http://www.chron.com/news/houston-texas/article/ No-one-told-Ford-tamales-need-to-be-unwrapped -1536700.php.

21 Wyatt Marshall, "How a Plate of Tamales May Have Crushed Gerald Ford's 1976 Presidential Campaign," *Munchies*, November 8, 2016, https://munchies.vice.com/ en/articles/how-a-plate-of-tamales-may-have-crushed -gerald-fords-1976-presidential-campaign.

22 Alex Katz, "Condoleeza Rice on growing up, Stanford and failing at piano," *The College Fix*, October 13, 2010, https://www.thecollegefix.com/post/3972.

23 "Mamie Francis Hafley, 1981 Cowgirl Honoree— Colorado," National Cowgirl Museum and Hall of Fame, http://www.cowgirl.net/portfolios/mamiefrancis-hafley.

24 "Kathleen McGinn Discusses Benefits to Children of Working Moms," YouTube video, 5:38, posted by CGTN America, October 2, 2015, https://www .youtube.com/watch?v=ATimBK0YsJQ.